D1604559

Front cover: view of Downtown Miami from Fisher Island.
© Thomas Delbek.

Back cover: New School of Architecture at the University of Miami Campus, Coral Gables.
Arch: Aldo Rossi with Morris Adjmi, 1987-92;
Preliminary sketch, 1987.
© Studio di Architectura, New York (photo:Ned Matura)

MIAMI

ARCHITECTURE OF THE TROPICS

MIAMI
ARCHITECTURE OF THE TROPICS

EDITED BY

MAURICE CULOT AND JEAN-FRANÇOIS LEJEUNE

FOREWORD BY

MARK ORMOND

INTRODUCTION BY

CAROLINE MIEROP

ESSAYS BY

MAURICE CULOT

ANDRES DUANY AND ELIZABETH PLATER-ZYBERK

JEAN-FRANÇOIS LEJEUNE

PRINCETON ARCHITECTURAL PRESS

Published in the United States
by Princeton Architectural Press, Inc.
37 East 7th Street — New York, New York 10003
212 - 995 - 9620

Miami - Architecture of the Tropics has been developed and edited by Maurice Culot
and Jean-François Lejeune, in collaboration with Caroline Mierop
and the initial help of Jean-Paul Midant;

based on the exhibition *Miami - Architecture of the Tropics,*
produced by the Fondation pour l'Architecture, Brussels, and by the University of Miami,
School of Architecture, shown at the Center for the Fine Arts, Miami, 1992.

Copy editors: Annabel Delgado, Roselyne Pirson.

Book design by Marc Gierst and Anne Gerard, La Page Sprl, Brussels, Belgium,
with Amanda de Selys.

Packaging by Luc Derycke, La Chambre Bvba, Gent, Belgium.

Copyright © 1993 by Archives d'Architecture Moderne, Brussels, Belgium.
Essays copyright © 1993 by Maurice Culot, Jean-François Lejeune,
Andres Duany & Elizabeth Plater Zyberk.
Introduction copyright © 1993 by Caroline Mierop.
Foreword copyright © 1993 by Mark Ormond.

Translations (from the French) by Pamela Johnston, Cleveland Moffett,
Angela Winchester, Jean-François Lejeune, Maurice Culot and Roselyne Pirson.

Captions copyright © 1993 by Archives d'Architecture Moderne.

Photographs copyright © 1993 by the individual photographers.

All rights reserved.
No part of this book may be published in any form
without written permission from the publisher.

PRINTED IN BELGIUM
ISBN: 1-878271-75-X
Library of Congress Cataloging-in-Publication
Data for this book is available
from the Publishers.

The metrorail bridge above
the Miami River,
at the entrance
to Downtown.
The neon lighting
is an installation
by the artist Rockne Krebs
and was installed under
the public program
Art in Public Spaces.

© Dade County Art in Public Spaces.

ACKNOWLEDGMENTS

We would like to thank THE SCHOOL OF ARCHITECTURE OF THE UNIVERSITY OF MIAMI
for its contribution to the organization of the exhibition and the book, particularly:
JORGE L. HERNANDEZ, Interim Dean & Assistant Professor,
JOSÉ GELABERT-NAVIA, Associate Professor & Interim Dean during the year 1990,
ELIZABETH PLATER-ZYBERK, Professor,

ROCCO J. CEO, Assistant Professor, for his help in organizing the exhibition for Brussels
and Groningen,
LYNN PARKS, Assistant to the Dean,
ROBERTO M. BÉHAR and TEOFILO VICTORIA for their architectural tours and their interpretation of
Miami,
JAN HOCHSTIM, for sharing his interest in Miami of the 50s and 60s,
ARISTIDES MILLAS, for his lectures on the architecture of Miami and his passion for historic postcards.

Our thanks go to the following institutions:

THE CENTER FOR THE FINE ARTS MIAMI, particularly MARK ORMOND, Director and
BRENDA WILLIAMSON, Associate Director for programs and communication,
THE DADE COUNTY ART IN PUBLIC SPACES, particularly VIVIAN RODRIGUEZ, Director,
THE HISTORICAL ASSOCIATION OF SOUTHERN FLORIDA, particularly ANDREW BRIAN, Director,
DAWN HUGH, Curatorial Assistant and REBECCA SMITH, Curator of Archival Materials,
THE MIAMI CHAPTER OF THE AMERICAN INSTITUTE OF ARCHITECTS, particularly ROBERT CHISHOLM,
President, and SUBRATO BASU, Member Board of Directors,
THE MIAMI DADE PUBLIC LIBRARY, particularly BARBARA YOUNG, Art Services,
THE CITY OF MIAMI OFFICE OF FACILITIES DEVELOPMENT,
THE DOWNTOWN DEVELOPMENT AUTHORITY MIAMI, particularly MATTHEW D. SCHWARTZ, Executive
Director and ADAM LUKIN, Urban Design Coordinator,
THE CITY OF CORAL GABLES, particularly CATHERINE B. SWANSON, Development Director, ELLEN
UGUCCIONI, Historic Preservation Administrator and MICHELLE SEBREE, Historic
Preservation Assistant,
THE CITY OF MIAMI BEACH,
THE MIAMI DESIGN PRESERVATION LEAGUE, particularly BERNARD ZYSCOVICH, Chairman,
THE WOLFSONIAN FOUNDATION, particularly PEGGY LOAR, Executive Director,
THE WOLFSON INITIATIVE, particularly CATHY LEFF, Director of Program Development.

And also:

STEVEN BROOKE and THOMAS DELBECK, for their photographic generosity and advices,
JAVIER CENICACELAYA for his support as Dean of the School of Architecture
during the year 1991-1992,
ROBERT DAVIS, for his hospitality in Seaside,
ANDRES DUANY and ELIZABETH PLATER-ZYBERK, for sharing their knowledge of American urbanism,

BETH DUNLOP, architectural critic at *The Miami Herald*, for her constant fight toward architecture excellence and quality of life in the City,
BILLY KEARNS, for his help and enthusiasm for Morris Lapidus,
VICTORIA LAGUETTE, for her help and her enthusiasm for Rufus Nims,
LYNN MILLER, for her help in Windsor Vero Beach,
ROSARIO MARQUARDT, for her friendly support,
CHARLES HARRISON PAWLEY, for his architectural tours and his index of Miami architects,
ROSELYNE PIRSON, for her editorial help and advice,
ROGIER VAN ECK, for his photographic reportage,
DEAN AND JANIA ZIFF, for their constant support and patronage of architecture and urbanism in Miami, for their direct contribution to the exhibition and book, and for their hospitality at Ca'Ziff.

Our thanks go also to the following architects:

CHARLES BARRETT, ROBERTO M. BÉHAR, LES BEILINSON, ROBERT BROWN and PAUL DEMANDT, ROBERT BRADFORD BROWNE, ROBERTO BURLE-MARX and CONRAD HAMERMAN, HILARIO CANDELA and MICHAEL KERWIN (Spillis Candela and Partners), EDDY CASTINEIRA, ROCCO J. CEO, JAIME CORREA, RAOUL and MARICÉ CHAEL, ANNABEL DELGADO and MARK HARRINGTON, VICTOR DOVER, ANDRES DUANY and ELIZABETH PLATER-ZYBERK, BERNARDO FORT-BRESCIA and CARLOS TOUZET (Arquitectonica International), JOSÉ A. GELABERT-NAVIA, MARIA DE LA GUARDIA and TEOFILO VICTORIA, MARK HAMPTON, RICHARD HEISENBOTTLE, JORGE L. HERNANDEZ, PETER JEFFERSON, MORRIS LAPIDUS, ROLANDO LLANES, DENIS HECTOR and JOANNA LOMBARD, TED HOFFMAN JR., TOMAS LOPEZ-GOTTARDI, SUZANNE MARTINSON, RONEY MATEU, SCOTT and ZOANNE MERRILL, JOHN NICHOLS (the Nichols Partnership), RUFUS NIMS, CHARLES HARRISON PAWLEY, RAFAEL PORTUONDO, HERVIN ROMNEY, GEORGE F. REED, THOMAS A. SPAIN, KENNETH TREISTER, JORGE, LUIS and MARI TERE TRELLES, ERIC VALLE, ROBERT WHITTON, BERNARD ZYSCOVICH,

and

MORRIS ADJMI and ALDO ROSSI (Studio di Architettura), STEVEN HOLL, PHILIP JOHNSON and JOHN BURGEE (New York); RODOLFO MACHADO and JORGE SILVETTI (Boston); LEON KRIER (London); S.U. BARBIERI (Studio di Architettura, s'Gravenhagen); GEORGES REUTER and LUCIEN STEIL (Luxemburg); HANS IBELINGS and RUDOLF BROUWERS (Stichting Nederland Instituut, Rotterdam), and all their collaborators for the material that they have generously lent to us.

To the photographers:
AL BARG, STEVEN BROOKE, THOMAS DELBECK and M. TEDESKINO, CARLOS DOMENECH, DAN FORER, PATRICIA FISHER, KATHRYN A. HALL, NORMAN MAC GRATH, RAUL PEDROSO/SOLO, ROLAND U. UNRUH and BACARDI IMPORTS (Miami); EZRA STOLLER-ESTO PHOTOGRAPHICS (Mamaroneck-New York), ROSANNA LIEBMAN, RICHARD PAYNE, PAUL WARCHOL (New York); ANTONIA MULAS, *THE ABITARE MAGAZINE* (Milan); ROGIER VAN ECK (Brussels) and SATELLITE MAPS INC.

Finally we thank MARILYN AVERY, GEOFF FERRELL, SCOTT HEDGE, XAVIER IGLESIAS, FRANK MARTINEZ, GEORGES PASTOR, JOHN ROCKWELL, ALAN SHULMAN, MARTIN CURI, CARLOS LANZA, RENÉ PUCHADES, EDUARDO VILLAREAL, GRAZIA GARRONE, MICHEL LOUIS, JEAN-PIERRE MAJOT, LAURELLA PAZIENZA, CHRISTINE MONET, ANNETTE NEVE, ARLENE DELLIS, STEVE MORGAN, ANA LLEONART-RODRIGUEZ,
and the entire staff of THE UNIVERSITY OF MIAMI SCHOOL OF ARCHITECTURE,
of THE CENTER FOR THE FINE ARTS MIAMI, of THE ARCHIVES D'ARCHITECTURE MODERNE, Brussels
and THE FONDATION POUR L'ARCHITECTURE, Brussels.

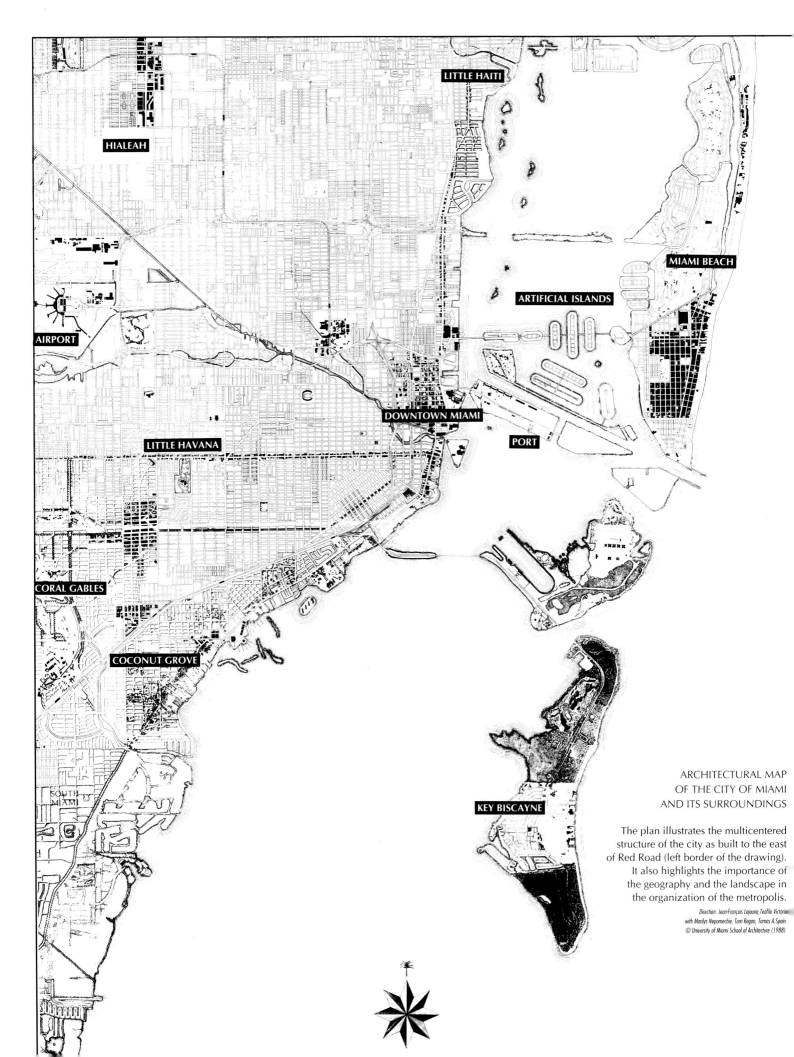

LITTLE HAITI

HIALEAH

MIAMI BEACH

AIRPORT

ARTIFICIAL ISLANDS

DOWNTOWN MIAMI

LITTLE HAVANA

PORT

CORAL GABLES

COCONUT GROVE

SOUTH
MIAMI

KEY BISCAYNE

ARCHITECTURAL MAP
OF THE CITY OF MIAMI
AND ITS SURROUNDINGS

The plan illustrates the multicentered
structure of the city as built to the east
of Red Road (left border of the drawing).
It also highlights the importance of
the geography and the landscape in
the organization of the metropolis.

Direction: Jean-François Lejeune, Teofilo Victoria
with Marilys Nepomechie, Tom Regan, Tomas A.Spain.
© University of Miami School of Architecture (1988).

CONTENTS

F O R E W O R D

M A R K   O R M O N D

Elevated plaza of the
Dade County Cultural
Center.
Facade of the main
Public Library.
Philip Johnson and
John Burgee, 1984.
© *Richard Payne.*

Downtown Miami:
detail of *Dropped
Bowl with scattered
slices and peels.*
Claes Oldenburg and
Coosje van Bruggen,
1990: a fountain in
the shape of orange
slices, installed through
the *Art in Public Spaces*
program initiated
in 1973.
In the background,
the first skyscraper in
Miami, the Dade County
Courthouse
Arch: A. Ten Eyck Brown
& August Geiger,
1928.
© *Dade County Art in Public Spaces.*

Miami... the word evokes sensations of clattering palm fronds, brilliant sunlight, cool water and humid hammocks. To invade a web of hammocks in Coral Gables or dense growths of ferns and palms in Coconut Grove would appear to be an unseemly intrusion of a settlement created by nature. Even the sea grass plains of marshland appear unsuitable for development.

This publication of *Miami — Architecture of the Tropics* reveals the extraordinary achievement of architects faced with the challenge of designing buildings to co-exist with the climate and topography of the tropics. Residential, commercial and institutional concerns of form and function are addressed in a great variety of design solutions. This history of architecture in Miami documents these parallel interests. In the best examples neither dominates. In the early part of the century, however, practical solutions to the demands of the tropical climate mandated a particular design to solve the need for basic human comfort. One must recognize the enormous impact of air conditioning, which provided a dramatic climatic alternative.

Miami in 1993 is a cosmopolitan centre where the built environment is a profound reflection of a city that considers itself a gateway to the world. While the needs of a client may be specific to South Florida, the options and interpretations provided by creative and innovative individuals are not only cognescent of historical precedent but also model solutions for other cities.

As an institution that promotes dialogue across all art forms and cultures, the Center for the Fine Arts recognizes the significance of this publication and the exhibition that inspired it.

T R A N S A T L A N T I C

CAROLINE MIEROP

© Antonia Mulas.

This book is a confession, or call it a discovery, a labor of love, a way of expressing what Maurice Culot has called "astonishment." It is the collective effort of a handful of architects and city-lovers, of Europeans from over here and from over there, brought together by chance friendships, shared experiences and beliefs, people with an appetite for the freedom and frankness that come through traveling, meeting others and the accidents of conversation.

The book is a homage to the New World, to the founding of cities, and specifically to Miami, nearly a century in the building and still under construction along that precarious line between terra firma and swampland, nature and artifice, the metropolis and the province, business and leisure, between the myth and the *faits divers*, North and South, vice and virtue. It is a homage, too, to Miami's tireless pioneers — Julia Tuttle and men like Brickell, Flagler, Deering, Munroe, Merrick, Fisher, Curtiss — as well as to today's generation of pioneers, the builders of the new communities, undaunted by hurricanes or economic crises.

The Bather.
Rosario Marquardt, 1990.
Pastel on paper.
© Collection of the artist.

This book is also an expression of thanks to all the architects, clients, promoters and backers, teachers and students, librarians, museum curators and archivists, painters and photographers — in a word, friends — who have invited us to their

15

city and made us feel welcome. They took the trouble to introduce us to a city that, in the eyes of a foreign visitor, can seem unapproachable, even hostile. When I landed there for the first time ten years ago for a mere 24 hours, I had wandered in a daze in search of the improbable centre of what seemed an infinite pistachio-colored suburb that stretched from the airport to the ocean.

In this transatlantic publishing venture, the University of Miami has played the role of catalyst. North American architects often suffer from what might be called a history complex; they tend to exploit the past, hence their fascination with Europe and the lands of older civilizations. This may also explain the extraordinary number of studies they have carried out on European cities. One has only to compare these with the relative paucity of similar research on American cities on this side of the Atlantic. Then there are the American summer schools in Rome, Venice, London, Paris, and the short-or long-term visiting professorships on campuses throughout the States. I held one of them myself at the University of Miami.

In Miami more than elsewhere the cultural hinterland can be regarded as extending all the way to Europe. Looked at from New England, Florida is little more than a province, a vaguely exotic cul-de-sac at the edge of the continent. But having chosen to take advantage of its status as a frontier and Atlantic port, Miami has become a bridgehead where the very density of international trade and traffic, the confusion of cultures and languages — English, Spanish, Creole — serve to keep alive its historic ties with the Mediterranean. The link is inscribed in many streets, neighborhoods and buildings of the city: Española Way, Granada Golf Course, Venetian Pool, Vizcaya, Casablanca Hotel, etc. And it is all the stronger for being at least partly invented out of a heritage that goes back to the far-distant Spanish occupation, a source continually enriched by waves of Latin immigration, from Cuba and Colombia, from Chile and Argentina.

House I, Cocoplum, Coral Gables. View of the loggia facing the city. Arch: Andres Duany & Elizabeth Plater-Zyberk, 1991. © Rogier Van Eck.

What a European who comes to Miami carries with him is, above all, the tangible proof of the cultural link, as well as an enthusiasm of appreciation that is largely uncritical (once the initial surprise is over). What the visitor from abroad sees spread before him is a work of imitation on the scale of an entire city. He is in an ideal position to evaluate the success of the peculiar made-in-Florida al-

The CenTrust Tower,
the second highest skyscraper
in the city.
The thirty-five floors of offices
seem to spring from an
eleven-floor podium
topped with a
roof garden and containing
parking and shops.
Arch: I.M. Pei, 1987.
In the foreground,
the Freedom Tower
Arch: Schulze & Weaver, 1926.

© Th. Delbeck & M. Tedeskino.

chemy that characterizes both architecture and everyday life, that blends the tropics, Europe and America, history and imagination, memory and the task at hand, pragmatism and make-believe, ingenuousness and know-how. The visitor discovers the headiness of a science-fiction adventure with a touch of casualness; the attractions of the Riviera minus the snobbery; the arrogance of the skyline with the ordinariness of the streets. He can find a garden city idealism, the uncompromising spirit of the avant-garde, a hint of classical elegance together with Caribbean color, light and shadow. In the end, he will recognize many of his own ideas, plans and ambitions transformed and reinterpreted on the scale and in the rhythm of another continent. The visitor is soon easily persuaded to leave behind the constrictions of taste and the intellectual inhibitions that affect one's judgment on the other side of the Atlantic. The debates about *faux-vieux* ("authentic reproductions"), copies and pastiche, that become so heated and inconclusive among architects in Europe — not to mention the antiques dealers — have no place in Miami. The entire city is meant to be a quote from the past; it integrates all the references, all the models that come together to forge its true identity. And it does so with the special aptitude that has always made American tradition so fertile. At the same time, the visitor finds none of the narrow-minded attitude — the blinkered notion of archeology — that would restrict the meaning of heritage and the importance of its preservation to only a certain range of dates. On the contrary, in Miami, there is a coexistence of architectural values from the 1920s, the would-be *Giralda* of Seville and the follies of the Chinese village in Coral Gables; then the Art Deco stucco of Miami Beach; the 1950s Moorish caryatids of the Casablanca Hotel; the Atlantis building of the 1980s by Arquitectonica; the Haitian market of 1990 by Charles H. Pawley. And they are already accepted as part of the common heritage; true symbols of local culture,

Inside the Haitian marketplace.
© *Charles Harrison Pawley.*

they form part of every advertising campaign for the city. In Europe today, the word "style" is taboo; at most, it may be used by art historians to refer to specific categories of the past; in Miami, architects regard style as an indispensable tool of their trade. They create variations on three basic themes, according to taste or the client's preference: the Mediterranean in all its variety, from classical to Costa-Brava kitsch; the so-called Florida Cracker style, named after the pioneer residents who came here during the mid-19th century building boom, and the "modern

Haitian marketplace
in Little Haiti
Arch: Charles Harrison
Pawley, 1989
© *Dan Fore*

18

style" in its rather frivolous local variant. No one would dream of attributing a superiority of inventiveness to any one of these schools, a more accurate reflection of the spirit of the times or of fitness to the environment. And yet, the critical sense is not absent; in fact, it is very lively and competition among architects is stimulating. Nothing is missing from the ongoing debate except the suggestion that any idea could be excluded a priori. At the same time, there is an overall frame of reference. In Europe, the principle of aesthetic standards in construction is a planning tool that has been discarded, not to say disqualified, because of its identification with a succession of recent dictators (Ceausescu of Roumania for one). In Miami, the principle is applied to entire neighborhoods. Whatever exceptions or compromises there may be, they do not interfere in any way with the original intention, which is to reinforce, or to create, the general harmony of the street, public space or new city. European architects can only envy the straightforwardness and promptness of a local administration that distributes an illustrated catalogue with examples of suggested materials for any given project. We can only applaud the kinds of initiatives that are tried and successfully concluded there which, over here, would be condemned to remain forever at the blueprint stage. Among many examples are the new cities designed in Miami by town planners Andres Duany and Elizabeth Plater-Zyberk who have flouted all the old habits, the conventional wisdom, not only with the compliance and encouragement of often quite famous architects, but with the full backing of investors and property developers.

It would be easy to list all the preconceived notions, all the old certitudes, that are either shaken or confirmed by contact with Miami. By simply observing the city and talking to the people who live there, the visitor from abroad is constantly struck by the different ways of thinking and doing, ways that astonish, inspire new ideas and give pleasure.

This book tries to suggest some aspects of this experience. We hope that the articles, photographs and drawings that follow will inspire readers to work out their own tour of the city, act as their own guides. For the European, the book is an invitation to voyage. For the people of Miami, it is a different kind of mirror, a new perspective, a portrait that has perhaps been a bit touched up and that is necessarily incomplete. We trust we will be forgiven for our decision (which could be interpreted as naive or wilfully blind) to relegate to the back of the book the examples of injustice, prejudice and violence that Miami suffers from.

The *Atlantis* apartments.
Arch: Arquitectonica
International, 1982.
© *Norman Mac Grath*

20

Ca' Ziff. The loggia on the second floor of the guest house.
Arch: Teofilo Victoria and Maria de La Guardia
with Tomas Lopez-Gottardi, 1987-92.

© Rogier Van Eck.

Yet, it is only by taking this reality into consideration that we can understand the broader context, the true perspective, and the sense of all-out commitment of the men and women who live there.

And so the myth and the tradition are handed on. May they continue to serve today as sources of courage and resolve when facing the difficulties ahead. For the third time in as many decades, Miami has been devastated by a powerful hurricane — few casualties, but thousands of houses destroyed and the city's spectacular natural landscape ruined and uprooted. A tragic episode, and yet, we may be certain, the first page of a new book that Miami has already begun to write.

The Bauhaus-style student dormitories, now housing the School of Architecture on the University of Miami campus.
Arch: Marion Manley, 1946.
In the foreground, a homeless shelter prototype designed and built by a group of students under the direction of the architect and professor Gary Greenan.
© Jean-François Lejeune.

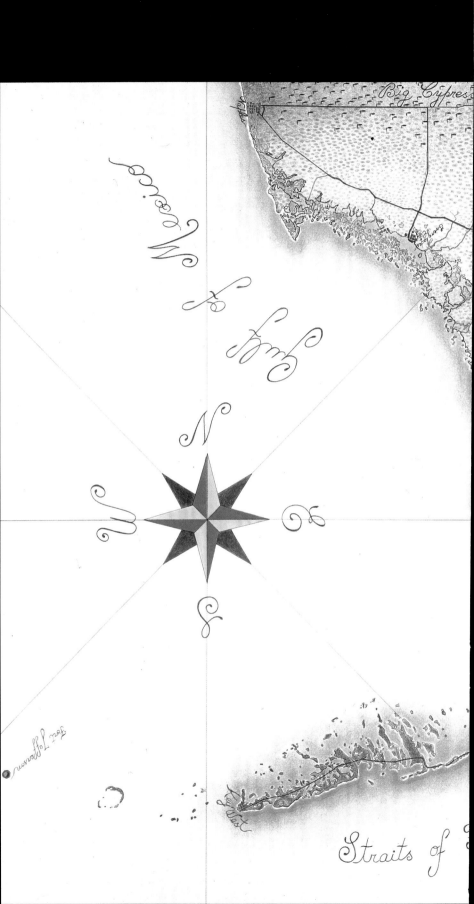

Big Cypress

Gulf of Mexico

N

W

E

S

Fort Jefferson

Straits of

Key West

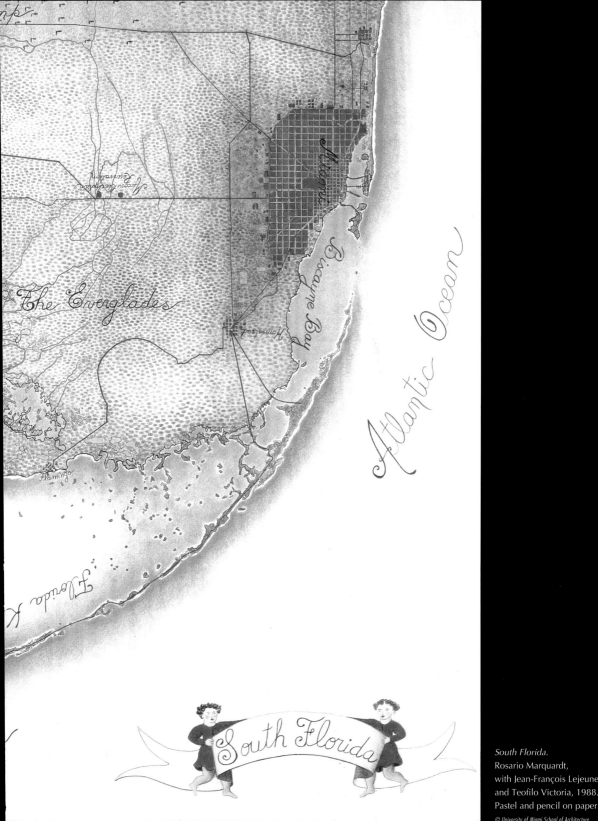

The Everglades

Miami

Biscayne Bay

Atlantic Ocean

Homestead

Flamingo

Florida K

South Florida.
Rosario Marquardt,
with Jean-François Lejeune
and Teofilo Victoria, 1988.
Pastel and pencil on paper.
© University of Miami School of Architecture

BLOWS TO THE HEART AND FLEETING IMPRESSIONS

MAURICE CULOT

The aerial atrium of the *Atlantis*.
Arch: Arquitectonica International,
1980-82.

© *Norman Mac Grath.*

Looking south on the
beach from a room in the
Fontainebleau Hotel in
1955. The cabanas and
the French gardens have
since been destroyed.

© *Historical Association of Southern Florida.*

Just a few years ago Miami was something of an unknown entity to Europeans —
even to seasoned travelers well acquainted with the cities, architecture, people
and spectacular landscapes of North America. While it was easy to picture other
cities — New York, Los Angeles, Chicago, even Kalamazoo, thanks to that song
that went around the world — Miami meant simply beaches, palm trees, and the
television series. To evoke the city's skyline, grand vistas, parks, monuments,
museums, and architecture required a concentrated effort.

Once past this hurdle, the images would begin to crowd onto the screen of
memory. First of all, scenes from the cinema. Marilyn Monroe in *Some Like it
Hot*. And that ultimate riposte... when Jack Lemmon, in drag, tells the multi-
millionaire who wants to marry him that he isn't a woman after all, and the
multi-millionaire replies, calmly and with a big smile, "Nobody's perfect."
Nobody's perfect could be the motto of all those European travelers who have
been waiting till now to discover Miami and revise their opinions of the city
which today can lay claim to being the most potent, poetic expression of the
American Dream of adventure, discovery, encounter.

For a long time the movies gave glimpses of a double-sided resort city. The Marx Brothers, Frank Capra, Billy Wilder, then television showed two types of inhabitant — hard-headed multimillionaires who strutted around like commodores, and imperturbable retired folks in sun vizors, who sat in serried ranks of easy chairs in pastel colors that matched the facades of their residential hotels. A map of Miami drawn around 1970 by European movie fans therefore would have shown two decorative styles. One part of the fictional resort would have consisted of grand mansions, large Mediterranean-style properties, golf courses and clubhouses, yachts, and elegant beaches — a whole world, with the generic name of Palm Beach, that took in every Boca Raton and Coconut Grove on the coastline of Florida. The other part would have been represented by a row of concrete shoeboxes with narrow facades covered in Art Deco signs, and views of the palm tree-lined Ocean Drive, with a band of slow-moving cumulus clouds outlined against a lapis lazuli sky, an endless beach, and a horizon too close to the equator to be troubled by the movement of tides — but sometimes hit by hurricanes, violent tropical storms.

To anchor this imaginary city in geographical space, the map-makers would have marked off its western boundary with an immense green smear bearing the inscription *Hic sunt crocodili*: the Everglades, familiar to Europeans through advertisements for a well-known aperitif showing a kind of ballet danced by spider-like machines propelled by immense fans which stir up the vast waters and reveal "hammocks" (floating islands of tropical jungle) and clumps of mangroves (the "mothers of islands") which stand upright on their roots like wading birds.

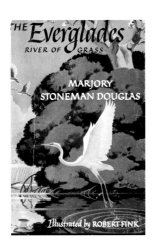

I learned some of the secrets of this vast area by reading the work of Marjory Stoneman Douglas, a historian, admirable woman, committed, sometimes militant ecologist, one-time centenarian, and author of *The Everglades, River of Grass*, first published in 1947 and reissued many times since. The Everglades — known to the Indians as *Pa-Hay-Okee* (grassy river) — cover some 2000 square miles, far less than their original expanse. They are rarely more than one foot deep, and are under constant threat, not only by periods of drought but by a disastrous drainage policy, by canals

Picking oranges in Florida. Postcard.
Private collection.

Mangrove tree. Sunny Isles, Miami Beach. Postcard.
© *Historical Association of Southern Florida.*

American Flamingo.
John James Audubon,
The Birds of America, Plate CCCCXXXI, 1838.
© *Historical Association of Southern Florida.*

Bahia Honda Bridge.
The highest span of the Overseas Highway
on the way to Key West, Florida.
Postcard.
In 1896, Henri Flagler
brought the railroad line to Miami
at the invitation of Julia Tuttle.
This is considered as the official birthdate of the city.
Flagler laid out tracks all the way to Key West.
The first train left Miami on January 22, 1912.
The railroad infrastructure was destroyed
by a hurricane on Labor Day, 1935.
Private collection.

which allow the infiltration of sea water, and, last but not least, by urbanization and real estate speculation. The idea of making the area a national park was first put forward in 1928 by the landscape architect Ernest F. Coe and realized twenty years later. To achieve this, it was necessary to negotiate with the native Americans, including the Miccosukees, who had never met an official representative of the United States government before 1935, had never been defeated by the Whites, and had never signed a treaty with the United States. In 1945 a Bureau of Indian Affairs census put their number at 684...

Going on through the box of memories, I come across a number of postcards from the 30s and 40s sent by some distant uncle from America. They are part of the "Tropical Florida" series, produced by the genuine patented "Curteich-Chicago Art-Colortone" process and immediately recognizable by their texture, like printed cloth, which lends them an undeniable artistic cachet.

I have before me a postcard of a railroad bridge disappearing into the ocean. I learned later that this was the line linking the different Keys with each other and the mainland. But here, for once, the reality did not live up to my expectations. I made a pilgrimage to Key Largo, in the footsteps of Humphrey Bogart and Lauren Bacall, to find that the Key had disappeared, drowned in the ribbon of insipid constructions lining the interminably boring highway that replaced the railroad, which was destroyed by a hurricane just a few years after it was brought into service.

Another view shows men perched on large ladders with bags across their shoulders, picking oranges rendered florescent by the magic of "Art-Colortone." These plantations, like those of Coral Gables in the 1920s, probably have been replaced by building lots. The stock market rose in the years following the First World War, but Miami real estate rose even faster. Marjory Stoneman Douglas wrote:

Trains, boats, automobiles arrived jammed with people. Hotel and rooming houses were packed. Tourists slept on porches, in tents, on park benches. The air was electric with talk of money. "Millions" became a common word. Business lots, house lots, buildings, houses, tracts at the edge of the city, and tracts beyond tracts began to sell and resell as fast as the papers could be made out. Sales were made with small down payments of cash and any number of mortgages. Paper profits were dizzy.

It was all cloudy, all visionary, all on paper, but everybody making these heady millions clung fiercely to the belief that it was real and that it would go on indefinitely.

Outside Miami subdivision after subdivision, to the very edge of the watery Glades, had their barbecues and advertisements and auctioneers bellowing to waiting crowds. Vast gateways were erected, through which sidewalks and street lights led to nothing at all but more land. Streets were laid out in the usual gridirons, with no other planning, no parkways, no parks, no provisions for anything but a quick turnover of money.[1]

In September 1926, Miami was devastated by a hurricane which killed around a hundred people, destroyed 2,000 homes, and seriously damaged 3,000 more.

This damage to property, however, appears slight in comparison with that caused by Hurricane Andrew which, in the night of August 24, 1992, destroyed some 25,000 homes, and heavily damaged 50,000 others in South Dade.

While Andrew claimed few lives, the hurricane of 1926 was deadly and wrecked the neighborhoods which symbolized the prosperity of the city, like Miami Beach and Coral Gables.

Back then, weather forecasters were unable to plot the precise course of the hurricane and give advance warning to the population — which consisted mainly of new arrivals who had no experience of hurricanes, and had certainly never read about them in the alluring brochures put out by the land agents. The damage was aggravated by the fact that many of the houses were not built solidly enough. The suddenness, violence, and spectacular impact of the

The Tides.
Ocean Drive,
Miami Beach.
Postcard.
Arch: L. Murray Dixon,
1936.
© Historical Association of Southern Florida.

hurricane of 1926 — the ships thrown out of the bay — struck imaginations and spelled the end of the property boom. For many years "Florida real estate" remained a subject for jokes. 1926 was a watershed for Florida in the same way that the Wall Street Crash of 1929 was a watershed for the rest of the country. The event remains engrained in the collective memory: bars and hotels still have photographs of the catastrophe — put there perhaps out of nostalgia, perhaps out of a desire to exorcise the forces of nature, which from time to time remind us of their power to thwart our best-laid plans.

Miami Hurricane of 1926.
The photograph dated the 19th of September
shows the destructions on Biscayne Boulevard
along the Bay.

© Historical Association of Southern Florida,
Photographer William O. Verne.

Pages 34-35:
A vision of New York
recaptured in Miami Beach:
looking south from
2Oth Street
along Collins Avenue.
Postcard.
© Historical Association of Southern Florida.

Hotel Carlton.
Collins Avenue, Miami Beach.
Postcard.
© Historical Association of Southern Florida.

Crescent Hotel.
Ocean Drive, Miami Beach.
Postcard.
© Historical Association of Southern Florida.

Collins Avenue, Miami Beach, Florida

The Breakwater.
Ocean Drive,
Miami Beach.
Arch: Anton
Skislewicz, 1939.

© Historical Association of
Southern Florida.

Postcards again. In bulk this time. Distributed free to promote Miami Beach hotels. The Hotel Carlton, 1433 Collins Avenue, with "Cedar Lined Closets in every Room." The Orleans Apartment Hotel, 18th Street, recommended for its "Pullmanettes." The Hotel Good on Ocean, which advertised a "European-plan dining room service, both table d'hôte and à la carte." The Corsair, First Street and Ocean, with "Elevator — Solarium — Spacious Terraces" all at "reasonable rates." The Dorset on Collins Avenue, "New modern 90-room hotel — near theaters and golf courses," and so on.

Miami is too vast, too unexpected, too rich in events, too changeable to be shown in postcards and summed up in the pages of a guidebook. Here the pleasures are directly related to the welcome you receive, to the things people show you rather than to the hypothetical tourist itineraries. And I've received such a consistently warm welcome, in the few years that I've been visiting regularly, that Miami has become one of my favorite cities, the one I miss when I'm away, the one I rediscover with the most pleasure. It arouses in me the same emotions as the Basque Country, with which it shares many ties.

Miami has the largest *pelota* facade in the world, and a sizable Basque community. If I had to recommend a theme to historians of modern architecture, I would not hesitate to suggest a study of the artistic and architectural exchanges between these two extreme territories which are united by a common geographical and historical fate — that of being at the same time within and outside a country, of being a population (if not a nation) apart, on the borders, in frontier territory.

Miami. I know of no other city in which traveling by automobile ignites such a festival of the senses, and no other lagoon city which offers so many perspectives on itself. Some memorable experiences:

Passing through the tunnels of greenery on the residential streets of Coral Gables. Taking a scenic detour overlooking a park and finding immense banyan trees with weird trunks and a tangle of roots dropping from their enormous trunks. The banyan's relative, the *Ficus aurea*,

U.S.1,
north of Miami.
Souvenir folder of Miami,
1926.
© *Historical Association of Southern Florida.*

The Venetian Islands under construction.
The causeway connects Miami Beach to Miami.
Postcard.

© Historical Association of Southern Florida.

Watson Island, the Port and Downtown Miami.

© Steven Brooke.

has an evil reputation for strangling the trees on which its supports itself—another reminder of what nature is capable of.

Driving along U.S.1., the highway which runs all the way from the Canadian border to the very end of Florida, Key West. As the road passes through Miami, it acquires a guard of honor made up of thousands of proud, elegant Royal palms. Beyond all this, there is the incredible quality of distance which characterizes the city landscapes. The sea-level causeways linking Miami with Miami Beach and the man-made islands in the bay, give a unique sense of intimacy with the water. We pass along the keyside, right by the bows of immaculate liners—I feel a moment of emotion as I recognize the ex- *France*, and see a leaping speedboat parallel us on the water.

The approach to the city centre via the high-level expressways is equally impressive. After the amphibious car, the flying automobile. The sweeping curves of concrete reveal a changing panorama of downtown: the skyscrapers seem to be pirouetting like giant fashion models in the landscape. This quality of distance unique to Miami has been exploited to the full in the work of Arquitectonica, which has a strong graphic impact and a distinct sculptural feel. In the tropics, the external image of the city assumes an importance which it cannot have in northern cities, and Arquitectonica can be labeled "100 percent functional / 100 percent artistic."

The inhabitants of Miami may be tired of wasting time in traffic jams and in queues at ill-conceived road junctions. As Beth Dunlop writes (in *The Miami Herald*, 22 May 1992): *Reason doesn't often prevail. We seem to powerless in the face of fast traffic, and then we have to go to extremes. We end up with barricades and guard houses and high walls and dead-end streets.* Despite this, and despite the plague of urban sprawl, Miami's elevated and seaborne highway infrastructures, including the new aerial metro, have an indisputable poetic power.

Is it possible to retain this poetry while combating pollution, environmental degradation, and the automobile's erosion of the quality of urban life? This problem is being addressed in various ways. With the best of intentions, engineers are building concrete safety walls

Downtown seen from the Miami River. In the foreground, the tables of the Big Fish Restaurant.
© Rogier Van Eck.

Site plan.

THE STAR OF MIAMI

Miami Centennial Project, 1896-1996.
Arch: Roberto M. Béhar,
with Fauziah Ab-Rahim, Rosario Marquardt, 1992.

The origin of this project is in the sky.

Like a shooting star that appears as a temporary streak of light, this proposal will first be seen from the air as one flies into Miami. From this point of view, the project will present itself as a park, that reunites the sea and the sky in the form of an island with the shape of the stars. This aerial perspective introduces the subject as a new kind of urban landmark, at the scale of the New City. The precise and particular outline of the intervention underlines the individuality of the project and highlights the identity of Miami: the Magic City.

Hammock entrance.

Plan.

Wall with hammock and palm trees.

41

along the causeways, although this may destroy the extraordinary ethereal sensation of driving along at water level. And a number of city planners, including Elizabeth Plater-Zyberk and Andres Duany, propose to reduce road traffic by reorganizing the city into communities (it has been calculated that each household in Miami currently makes an average of thirteen trips by car a day).

"Deco Delights" is the name of a chocolate cake topped with fresh cream and scoops of ice cream which used to be served in the Cardozo Hotel café in Miami Beach in the 1970s. *Deco Delights* is also the title of one of the many books devoted to the architecture of Miami Beach in the last fifteen years or so, since the formation of the Miami Design Preservation League and the official dedication of the unique Art Deco district. Much of the credit for this must go to Barbara Baer Capitman, linchpin of the preservation league and author of the aforementioned book. The streamline style Cardozo Hotel, a product of the prolix genius of Henry Hohauser, has been a feature of the grand architectural parade of Ocean Drive since its construction in 1939.

I go along Ocean Drive to the News Café on the corner of 8th Street, famous for its fruit salad and *piña colada* lunches, to meet Roberto Behar, the grandson of Jacques Behar, founder of the first modern Jewish armed force and paterfamilias of a clan which sees Buenos Aires as a suburb of Paris or New York, or vice-versa. Roberto Béhar teaches at the University of Miami School of Architecture.

Si te alejas acuerdate de mi. Monument for a Mexican-American neighborhood at corresponding San Diego Expressway Exit. Oil, wood, cardboard, tin, and papier maché model. Arch: Roberto M. Béhar with Rosario Marquardt, 1988.

An Argentine, he has a particularly acute perspective of Miami's geographical significance, seeing the city as the capital of a new world, a crucible which mixes the feelings, hopes, illusions of the New World and the Old, and then adds the Caribbean... a capital open to the south but at the same time a frontier town facing north: "City Lights," "Frontier Adventures"— or "America's Casablanca," as the headline in *Newsweek* on January 25, 1988 put it. Florida, the fourth populated state after California, New York and Texas, is discovering that it has a vocation for the movie business, for welcoming

Ocean Drive at night.
© Th. Delbeck & M. Tedeskino.

The Albion.
James Avenue, Miami Beach.
Arch: Igor Polevitsky, 1939.
© Historical Association of Southern Florida.

international fashion, for taking in Contra leaders, drug barons and "King Pins," and for accommodating members of the National Rifle Association.

Miami Beach is not just a stretch of sand but an island. It is the most liberal city in Florida, thanks to a massive influx of Jews from New York in the 1930s. In contrast, Miami is ultraconservative — it is the first city in the United States to have named an avenue after Ronald Reagan. Voting mainly follows ethnic lines: the Jews vote Democrat and the Cubans are overwhelmingly Republican. Cuban immigration is also uniquely political, large-scale and urban, in contrast to the economic and rural exodus of the Mexicans and Puerto Ricans. Cubans account for approximately 650,000 of the 900,000 Hispanics living in the twenty-eight municipalities of Dade County. They include 150,000 Marielitos, so called from their port of embarkation in Cuba, Mariel.

The Cubans were welcomed by President Jimmy Carter as a gesture of defiance to Castro, who used the opportunity to empty his jails of all prisoners detained under common law. The Hispanics also include about 80,000 Nicaraguans, who reinforce the political power base of the Cubans. Then come the other most important nationalities: Colombians, Salvadorians, Puertoricans, Dominicans, and about 80,000 refugees from Haiti.[2] Quite a contrast to the chilly Europe of the Common Market. Here, each immigrant is welcomed as a potential consumer, though the efforts made by city and county officials to assist the new arrivals are not always appreciated by the perpetually disadvantaged Afro-American population.

In contrast to Rio de Janeiro or Los Angeles, most of Miami's immigrants are politically conservative. The new arrivals, by virtue of their numbers and their refugee status, play a direct role in the political, cultural, and social life of the city. In the past, it took the Italians, Irish, and Portuguese two or three gener-ations to gain any position of power, but now the Cubans acquire citizenship after five years of legal residence and enter the American Dream on an equal footing.

Another difference from past immigrants is that the new generation born in the United States has not lost its language and culture.

Miami (from the Indian word for "fresh water") has sun, sand... and real estate speculation: architects, investors, and hoteliers refer to the pages of *Miami Today*, for information on real estate transactions, city planning, the state of the

Original sketch for Douglas Entrance, Coral Gables.
Arch: Walter De Garmo, Denman Fink, Phineas Paist, 1925-27.

© *Historical Association of Southern Florida.*

Curtiss' administration building is now the City Hall of Opa-Locka,
one of the poorest black communities in the city.
It was restored by Les Beilinson Architect in 1988.

Administration Building.
Sharazad Avenue, Opa-Locka.
Arch. and drawing: Bernhardt Müller, 1926.

© *Otto G. Richter Library, University of Miami.*

market, and profiles of VIP bankers and investors. But despite this, Miami is not a large city in the usual sense, but rather a series of experiences accessible in less than ten minutes by car.

The first thing to do when you get off the airplane is to turn to the section in the "Yellow Pages" which features Miami as "The City that Dreams Built." This compact, valuable guide tells you, should you need to know, how to obtain citizenship and establish legal residency; but essentially it gives a succinct outline of the various neighborhoods and communities of Miami. *Coconut Grove*, with its "chic boutiques and quaint cafés." *Coral Gables*, still "one of the most beautiful areas to call home." The *Art Deco District* with its "rounded corners, racing stripes, concrete eyebrows, and glass block." *Hialeah/Miami Springs* with the oldest and largest Basque *pelota* facade in the country. *Little Haiti,* the former *Lemon City*, and the *French Creole* quarter. *Little Havana*, the focus of the Cuban community: "Here, piñatas and plantains, guayabera shirts, cigarmakers, domino players, and outside cafés are at home on bustling Calle Ocho (SW 8th Street)." *Miami Beach, Miami Lakes, Miami Shores*: the names speak for themselves. *Opa-Locka*, a development built in the Moorish style by aviator Glenn Curtiss, who had apparently been much impressed by the sets of the *Thief of Baghdad. Overtown*, the black neighborhood, torn down out by urban redevelopment in the 1960s. And *Downtown Miami.*

Miami was founded barely 100 years ago. It was 1896 when Flagler brought the railroad into the town and later across the sea toward Key West (Flagler's Folly). The highway did not come until 1915. Miami, we have been warned, is a mass of different locations and communities impossible to explore all at once. And alongside the daytime city exists a second city of the night.

You can reach these experiences in less than ten minutes by car, but you have to choose what to see depending on the time you have available, your tastes, and your physical stamina.

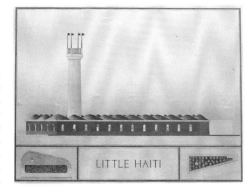

Little Haiti. Monument for the Haitian Quarter in Miami. A symbol of Haitian landscape and magic reaching Miami. Arch: Roberto M. Béhar, with Fauziah Ab-Rahim, 1985.

My choice is the architectural dreams of the builders of the city, both in the past, and in the present day, as evoked by Jean-François Lejeune later in this book. I would add also that I am not immune to the charms of the tropical night.

Coral Gables House.
Coral Way, Coral Gables.
© Rogier Van Eck.

In 1899 Doctor Solomon Merrick,
a Massachusetts Congregational minister,
purchased a 160-acre tract of land
located near newly founded Miami.
Reverend Merrick
and his son George settled in a log cabin
already standing on the property
and planted grapefruit and vegetables on their land.
The rest of the Merrick family soon
came to live on the Florida property,
which they called "Guavonia" after the fruit that grew there.
They lived in a newly constructed frame house
which was incorporated into the larger home.
Completed in 1906 and called "Coral Gables",
this house was built of native limestone rock
quarried from a nearby site, now the Venetian Pool.
As Merrick's crops prospered, more land was acquired,
bringing the plantation to about 1,600 acres
where George Merrick envisioned and later
developed a new Mediterranean-style community.
It was named "Coral Gables" after the home.

"WHEN THE MOON SHINES IN CORAL GABLES"
(Song popular in Coral Gables in the 1920s).

Coral Gables was founded in 1921 on agricultural land then far removed from the winter resorts of the Florida coast.

Its founder, a visionary and poet called George Merrick, was assisted by an architect (Phineas E. Paist), a landscape gardener (Frank Button), and an artist (Denman Fink). The 1926 hurricane and the Great Depression combined to ruin Merrick and prevent him from completing his project. But even incomplete, Coral Cables can still claim the title of the "most beautiful garden city in the world."

By 1927 Merrick was being harassed by creditors, but King Alfonso XIII of Spain, who was enthusiastic about anything that would give his country back a sense of the grandeur and influence it had once enjoyed, poured a little balm on Merrick's heart by bestowing upon him the Order of Queen Isabella of Castille "in appreciation and gratitude for choosing the Spanish style of architecture in building Coral Gables."

The houses, hotels, and public and commercial buildings in the Spanish style, together with those in the Colonial, French, Moroccan, Venetian, or even Chinese styles, are all fresh, inventive interpretations of images borrowed principally from the architectural repertoire of the Mediterranean and freely adapted to meet the requirements of the American way of life. Coral Gables constitutes an original and authentic work which draws inspiration from the patina of buildings and never descends to the level of kitsch, which is content merely with borrowed symbols and decoration.

To compensate for the distance from the beaches, Merrick constructed a network of canals served by gondolas, which allowed him to advertise "Forty Miles of Waterfront" Denman Fink converted a limestone quarry into a spectacular swimming pool, the "Venetian Pool," where Paul Whiteman stood on a raft, dressed in a bathing suit, and conducted his orchestra.

The "Spanish style," which here encompasses all Mediterranean cultures, allowed architecture to be conceived in the form of

The Miami Biltmore,
Coral Gables.
The main entrance.
Arch: Schultz & Weaver.
Drawing: Chester B. Price.
John McEntee Bowman,
The Miami Biltmore,
New York, 1926.
© *Historical Association of Southern Florida.*

Granada entrance,
Coral Gables.
Souvenir folder of Miami,
1926.
© *Historical Association of Southern Florida.*

picturesque tableaus. Its additive and asymmetrical designs also accommodated the complex demands of modern living with far greater ease than the formal mold of Classicism.

The local coral stone (actually an oolite) used in the first buildings was rapidly abandoned in favor of plaster, which required less skilled workmanship. Buildings could also be given an instant patina of age by beating the plaster with chains and brushing it with cow dung.
Coral Gables is entered through gates imitated from some Spanish or Mexican fortified town. Fountains embellish its squares. And in some places there are "villages," a somewhat exaggerated term for groups of individual houses built in different styles: Chinese, French, South African, Italian, etc.

Alcazar, Alcala, Alcantara, Andalusia, Asturias... from A to Z, the street names of Coral Gables comprise a list of famous cities or persons, mainly from Spain[3.] The story is that George Merrick's wife and family spent hours searching for appropriate street names, and found them mainly in the writings of Washington Irving (*The Alhambra, Conquest of Granada*, etc.)

The foliage of the banyan trees transforms the avenues into tunnels, while the palm trees — fully grown in less than ten years — display their abundant variety in courtyards, patios, and gardens: the Sabal palm (which can reach a height of sixty feet), the coconut tree, the royal palm, and many palmettos, including the much loved traveler's tree, so called because it retains water in its petioles.

In the centre of Coral Gables is the Biltmore Hotel with its *Giralda*-style tower[4]. This is one of three *Giraldas* built in Miami in the 1920s: the second one tops Freedom Tower in Downtown Miami: the third one, now destroyed, was part of the Roney Plaza Hotel on Miami Beach. A country club, golf course, and open-air swimming pool adjoin the hotel, which is centred around a paved courtyard lined with bars and restaurants.

Another bar, on the 14th floor, offers panoramic views. As evening falls, Coral Gables disappears into the night, hidden by the foliage which masks houses, lampposts, and even car headlights. At this time George Merrick's city becomes an island of shadows in the midst of an immense tapestry of points of light.

Traveler's Tree.
Rocco Ceo, 1991.
© Rocco Ceo.

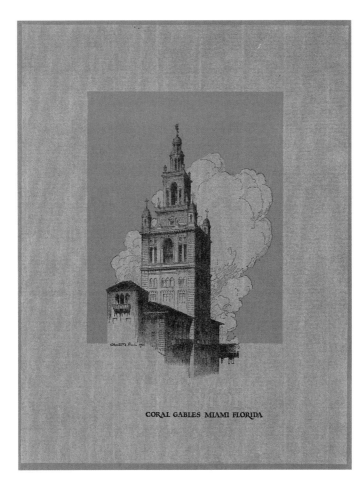

CORAL GABLES MIAMI FLORIDA

The Miami Biltmore,
Coral Gables.
Arch: Schultz & Weaver.
Drawing: Chester B. Price.
John McEntee Bowman,
The Miami Biltmore,
New York, 1926.
© Historical Association of Southern Florida.

Banyan tree in Coconut Grove.
Postcard.
© Historical Association of Southern Florida.

The Miami Biltmore,
Coral Gables.
The service building and
hotel group.
Arch: Schultze & Weaver.
Drawing: Chester B. Price.
John McEntee Bowman,
The Miami Biltmore,
New York, 1926.
© Historical Association of Southern Florida.

The Freedom Tower
facing the port
and Biscayne Bay.
Originally built as
the newspaper plant of
The Miami Daily News,
it was used in the 1960s
as an immigration centre
for Cuban refugees.
Arch: Schultze & Weaver,
1926.
Restoration:
Richard J. Heisenbottle
Architects, 1990.
© Dan Forer.

Biltmore Hotel.
The main lobby.
Coral Gables.
Arch: Schultze & Weaver,
1925.

© City of Coral Gables.

Interior of the Gusman
Center for the Performing
Arts on Flagler Street
Downtown Miami
The most beautiful
performance hall
in the city
originally built for the
motion pictures
Arch: John Eberson, 1926.
Restoration
Richard J. Heisenbottle
Architects

© Dan Forer

"PEOPLE WHO LIVE IN GLASS HOUSES SHOULD PULL DOWN THE BLINDS"
(A. Mizner, *Cynic's Calendar of Revised Wisdom*, 1900).

Predating Merrick's work at Coral Gables is that of the architect and entrepreneur Addison Cairns Mizner (1872 - 1933). From 1917 onward, Mizner was responsible for making the Spanish style popular amongst the wealthy, snobbish clientele of Palm Beach, which was being marketed as a winter resort by Paris Singer, heir to the sewing machine fortune. The term "Spanish style" does not convey the full semantic range of the architecture, which takes in all of the Mediterranean cultures, acclimates them and brings them together in the 20th century in the part of the New World formerly under Spanish influence. More than a "style," the term suggests "romance".

The joint Mizner-Singer enterprise was an immediate success. Mizner set up his own construction business to meet the growing demand for large residences in the Spanish style, and in 1925 he began, independently of Singer, to work on Boca Raton, a "city of red tiles" focused around the *Castillo del Rey*, a 1,000-room hotel.

When asked by Paris Singer about a suitable architecture for Palm Beach, Mizner replied: *A Moorish tower, like on the south coast of Spain, with an open loggia at one side facing the sea, and on this side a cool court with a dripping fountain in the shade of these beautiful palms.* And concerning the Everglades Club which Singer planned to build on the shore of Lake Worth:
A nunnery, with a chapel (the grand hall of the restaurant) built into the lake... a mixture built by a nun from Venice, added onto by one from Gerona, with a bit of new Spain of the tropics. The Carstairs residence (Palm Beach, 1920) was designed in the image of "a farmhouse of the Ferdinand and Isabella period;" and *Playa Riente*, a gigantic house which disappeared before preservation leagues existed, was inspired by a vision of an "old Gothic palace built out into the sea."[5]

Elevated plaza of the Dade County Cultural Center. On the left, the entrance to the Historical Association of Southern Florida. Arch: Philip Johnson and John Burgee, 1984.
© *Richard Payne.*

Mizner died bankrupt in 1933. Subsequently the Spanish style suffered both on account of its success and its use in less costly developments. It was also accused of not expressing the national character.

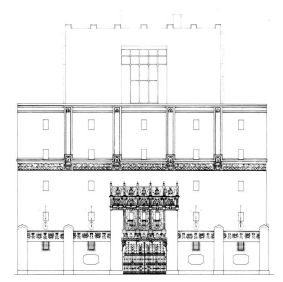

Elevation on
Washington Avenue
after renovation.
© Mark Hampton.

WOLFSONIAN FOUNDATION.
Formerly the Washington Storage Building.
Washington Avenue, Miami Beach.
Arch: Robertson & Patterson, 1927.
Renovation: Mark Hampton, with William S. Kearns, 1994.
The building will house a gallery for
permanent exhibition of the Mitchell Wolfson Jr. Collections
of Decorative and Propaganda Arts, a gallery for temporary exhibitions,
and a library and research centre. The original structure with its plateresque portal
inspired by the University of Salamanca has been renovated, and two additional floors
have been added on the roof. The interior, completely rebuilt, highlights spectacular decorative
and architectural pieces such as the reconstructed terracotta facade of a movie house
in Pennsylvania.
© Mark Hampton.

The entrance portal
before renovation.
© Steven Brooke.

At the end of the 70s, a rediscovery of Mizner's work inspired a revival of the Spanish style in Southern Florida, although this was usually limited to a few external symbols and isolated structures rather than the large-scale building of the 20s. There were, however, some noteworthy new projects: the Dade County Cultural Center with its various buildings grouped around an elevated courtyard by architects Johnson and Burgee, and the additions to the City Hall and Municipal Library of Boca Raton by Gee and Jenson. An inspiration in his own time, Mizner has once again become a point of reference for a new generation of architects.

I have spent a total of three months in Miami, spread over four visits of unequal length. This is not much time to become intimately acquainted with such a vast city, but it is long enough in that the days and nights were lived with intensity, thanks to friends.

We made our way through the cosmopolitan night. Clubs, restaurants, hotels, and bars provided rallying points in the exploded centre, fixing the web of the city by night. These were places with a lingering presence — where Ernest Hemingway or Paul Morand might come walking back through the door at any moment. These were nights full of questions about the way people act, and of stories that escape the teller by the light of day.

The woman with the tired hands whom we met one evening in Doc Dammers Saloon in Coral Gables was the daughter of a former German army officer who emigrated to Florida. We learned that by day she works in real estate, a traditional local profession, but by night she becomes a huntress at the wheel of her Cadillac. Her prey — any traveling businessman with a physique like Jack Palance. This was one encounter among many. Doc Dammers is located in the precincts of the Colonnade Hotel on the corner of Miracle Mile and Ponce de Léon Boulevard (called after the conquistador who discovered Florida in 1513). The club is decorated throughout with photographs which evoke Coral Gables and the personality of "Doc" Dammers, one of the most famous

Versailles, the landmark café-restaurant on SW 8th Street (Calle Ocho).
© *John Rockwell.*

Park Central Hotel.
Ocean Drive,
Miami Beach
Arch: Henry Hohauser,
1937.

© Th. Delbeck & M. Tedeskino.

63

CAFÉ
TU TU
TANGO
COCOWALK

Miami skyline at night.
© Steven Brooke.

THE ART OF PASTA

THE COLONNADE
HOTEL

auctioneers of the boom era. We can still hear the greeting of the tireless bar-maid, a warm, sparkling blonde with a strong Georgian accent, as we walked in the door, "Hi Guys."

Nighttime is the time for embracing Miami and tasting the fullness of the city, for moving on, untiring, through its unique world of contrasts and changes.

Versailles on the neon-bright Calle Ocho. A noisy Cuban restaurant in an old gas station which earns its name from the mirrors covering its walls from top to bottom. Apart from the house cocktails, *Mojito* and *Tropical Breeze* everything comes with black beans and plantains — fried, mashed, green bananas or yuccas of unforgettable insipidity. The exiles in the bar rail at Castro, comment on his latest speech, and imagine turning Havana into a suburb of Miami.

Still on Calle Ocho, this time at the junction of 23rd Street: Casablanca. Humphrey Bogart — an inescapable presence in Miami — and gastronomic curiosities... *Guarapo*, a juice obtained from pressed sugar cane; *Malta Hatuey*, a dark mixture made of water, malt, corn, caramel, and hops, no less. For dessert there is *Tres Leches*, a sweetish mixture of condensed milk, evaporated milk, and cream. A characteristic Latin ambience: the garish light from long neon tubes, the swishing of fans (Hunter, unmistakably), the Cuban and Colombian waitresses in pink aprons with black trim.

Heading south. A club on Dixie Highway. "Lipstick: Sophisticated Adult Enter-tainment." An advertisement for lascivious women. We take the precaution of wearing dark glasses, but see a show with a friendly, almost domestic complicity between the dancers and the regulars. Let's not be prudes. Miami certainly has its "hard" places. It's as easy here as anywhere else to "take a walk on the wild side, babe." All the same, I fear that tropical nature needs no lessons in lasciviousness from anyone.

Mac's "Club Deuce" Bar,
Miami Beach.
Postcard.
© Bob Kuebler, RGK Enterprises, Inc.

Back to Miami Beach. In the heart of the Art Deco District, between 5th and 15th streets: Ocean Drive, Collins and Washington avenues... where establishments spring up and fade from one season to the next. The oldest already have the status of classics. These include The Strand, the Coupole, and the Century Hotel, built in 1939 and considered to be one of the most representative examples of the work of the architect Henry Hohauser. The Century was acquired in 1988 by David Colby and Wilhelm Moser, publishers of the magazines *Select* and *The Manipulator*. Now successfully restored to its original condition, it accommodates the many fashion teams who come here to take springtime photographs in December.

Frequenting the clubs, hotels, and restaurants of Miami Beach provides an entertaining means of learning a little American history, because of the numerous theme decorations. One example is the WPA Restaurant, recently opened on Washington Avenue, where the frescoes on the walls recall the era of the "Works Progress Administration," one of the many programs initiated by Franklin D. Roosevelt to counteract the socio-economic effects of the Great Depression. One learns, just by reading the menu, that the WPA was responsible not only for the building of bridges, dams, and libraries, but for the creation of great works of public art, literature, theatre, and film. During its eight-year existence, billions were spent for the public good, and more than eight million people were returned to work.

No night out would be complete without a visit to Deuce — a place of lone women, drifters, creatures with lioness haircuts, Whites, Blacks, Latins, where all kinds of tensions are deflected from violence by fatigue, alcohol, and curiosity. A blue, red, and green neon sign showing the two of clubs (deuce). Black ceilings, black walls.
A man looks in from outside; he is naked. It's two in the morning by the octagonal clock encircled in green neon. Mac's "Club Deuce" Bar is on the corner of 14th Street and a Miami Beach back alley. Its 1930s interior makes it, as one reads on a postcard, "a popular tourist attraction as well as a friendly neighborhood gathering place." Why not, after all?

Back to Coral Gables and the nth stop for Cuban coffee served in a plastic thimble at an outside counter.

The dawn is a poignant curtain-raising on the day, violet-red and purple, as violent as a jet of colored ink. It brings us back to Denny's for a breakfast of pancakes covered with honey, scrambled eggs, sausages and ham, all washed down with tasteless coffee.

Century Hotel.
Ocean Drive,
Miami Beach.
Arch: Henry Hohauser,
1939.
© Jean-François Lejeune.

Gardens.
© Jean-François Lejeune.

Aerial view of Villa Vizcaya in 1963.
The Villa was built for James Deering,
a Maine-born man who made his fortune in
the manufacturing of farming machinery.
Arch: Francis Burrall Hoffman and
Paul Chalfin, 1914-16.
Gardens: Diego Suarez.
© Historical Association of Southern Florida.

CA ZIFF

Ca'Ziff. Atrium. Miami, 1989-1992
Arch: Teofilo Victoria & Maria de La Guardia,
with Tomas Lopez-Gottardi
Drawings: Maria de la Guardia, Teofilo Victoria

© Teofilo Victoria & Maria de La Guardia.

Dean & Jania Ziff Diptych.
Rosario Marquardt, oil on paper, 1986.

Collection Jania Victoria & Dean Ziff. © Rosario Marquardt.

VIZCAYA! An elevated Renaissance villa built by a super rich industrialist called James Deering (1859-1925) — the counterpart to William Randolph Hearst's California castle.

The villa, now the most visited monument in Miami, dominates Biscayne Bay. In front of it is a stone vessel which acts as a wharf and maybe as a breakwater. Surrounding it are gardens designed by Diego Suarez (1888-1971), who took unusual care to integrate it into the tropical vegetation.

The composition of the mansion impresses as much for itself as for the avowed intentions of its owner. There is an echo of its architecture in a house recently built nearby — the Ca'Ziff, home of Jania and Dean Ziff. But in place of the ostentation, theatricality, Renaissance taste, and fine arts spirit of the older house, the Ca'Ziff presents a metaphor for the house, the family, and their guests. The new house is an instrument with which to construct an architectural language, a dialogue between sky and water, vegetation and climate. The square skylight over the rainwater pool looks onto the stars as they pass through the twelve phases of the zodiac.

The gravity of the individual is confronted with the inexpressible, the joy of living amongst one's family and friends. One of the bedrooms bears the name of Pavarotti, who slept there after a memorable soirée held by Ziff's parents, Sanford and Helen, in aid of the Miami Concert Assocation. The elder Ziffs have also made a decisive pledge toward the construction of a new building for the University of Miami School of Architecture: a square 100-foot tower designed by Milanese architect Aldo Rossi.

Though a young city, Miami has many patrons of the arts. One of the most original, Mitchell Wolfson Jr., has maintained the traditional link between Europe and North America by creating simultaneously in Genoa and Miami two museums to house his collections of Decorative and Propaganda Arts. A con-

firmed bachelor, he founded the 200 + 1 Club, whose members comprise 200 women and one man. His intention is to create a sympathetic but active environment which would have a positive influence on the government of the city.

The Foundlings Club is located in the Sterling Building, one of the finest Art Deco commercial

Sterling Building. Lincoln Road Mall, Miami Beach. Arch: Alexander Lewis, 1928 and V.H. Nellenbogen, 1941.
© Th. Delbeck & M. Tedeskino.

buildings on Lincoln Road, the once prestigious commercial street built by Carl Fisher, and remodelled as a pedestrian mall in the 50s by Morris Lapidus, master INXS ("in excess," according to the formula learned from Victoria Laguette) of hotel architecture.

But, returning to the current scene, Charles Harrison Pawley is one of the best eclectic tropical architects in Miami, with a natural gift for always hitting on the right tone and solution for the contexts in which he is asked to build. I am indebted to him for having drawn my attention to several architects and practices.[6]

In the first instance there is Rufus Nims, who responded to the tropical environment with fine, inventive buildings which work comfortably without air conditioning and take account of natural ventilation and light filtered through vegetation. Nims has influenced three generations of architects, both through his ideas and his built works. Among those who have taken up his spiritual lead are the late Robert Bradford Brown, George F. Reed, Milton C. Harry, Peter Jefferson, the most inspired and most fantastic of the group of tropical architects, William Cox, a specialist in leisure architecture, and the flamboyant, anti-dogmatic Wilfredo Borroto.

Among the great architects who have passed away are:
F. Burrall Hoffman Jr., the architect of the Villa Vizcaya, an exemplary adaptation of the Mediterranean style to the tropical climate; Walter De Garmo, the most admired architect of the 30s and a master of the Mediterranean style; Maurice Fatio, well known for his buildings in Palm Beach and for the Indian Creek Country Club in North Miami Beach, one of the most elegant examples of the Mediterranean style in Miami; Marion Manley, designer, in 1946, of the immaculate Bauhaus-inspired residences that now house the School of Architecture; Russel T. Pancoast, one of the best loved of Miami's early architects, who founded the influential practice of Pancoast, Ferendino, Grafton, Spillis & Candela; Igor B. Polevitsky, a little-known giant of Modern architecture; Thurston Hatcher, who built houses with refined details in the spirit of Frank Lloyd Wright; and Herbert H. Johnson, a leading exponent of Modernist commercial architecture, who designed Bal Harbor Shops, the best shopping centre in Florida.

The Alhambra, a mixed-use complex, has as its centrepiece the Hyatt Regency Hotel, adjoined to a 14-story office tower. Alhambra Circle, Coral Gables. Arch: The Nichols Partnership, 1987.
© Martin Fine, Mark Surloff and Tom Knibbs.

The Colonnade. Miracle Mile & Ponce de Léon Boulevard, Coral Gables. Arch: Spillis Candela & Partners, Inc. (Aramis Alvarez), 1988.

The old Colonnade Building, originally used as headquarters of the Coral Gables Corporation, was designed in 1925 by the architects Phineas Paist, Walter De Garmo and Paul Chalfin. The new Colonnade incorporates the landmark and its elliptical rotunda within a mixed-use project containing a retail galleria, office space, a luxury hotel and a parking garage.
© H. Durston Saylon.

72

Back to our contemporaries:

Barry Sugerman; Jorge Arango, also an eloquent and respected critic; Mark Hampton, an uncompromisingly Modern tropical architect; Robert Whitton; Jaime E. Borrelli, Modernist Latin architect of the City Hall and Police Headquarters in Miami Beach; Kenneth Treister, a Renaissance man — architect, sculptor, photographer, and historian (author of a notable study of Art Nouveau in Nancy).

Hilario Candela represents commercial architecture at its best; his Colonnade is my favorite hotel after the Biltmore, not only for pleasant moments spent in Doc Dammers Saloon, but for its silhouette in the moonlight and its balance between rationalism and the Mediterranean style. Equally, there is the work of John R. Nichols, a prolific hotel architect. I particularly like the elevated terrace with swimming pool at the Alhambra (Hyatt Regency Hotel), where Nichols has created the ambience of a modern Mediterranean square within the heart of a monumental hotel complex. For architect Bernard Zyscovich, chairman of the Miami Design Preservation League, the Alhambra is a more "predictable" piece of architecture than the Colonnade Hotel or the Columbus Centre (architects: Mitchell and Giurgola with the Nichols Partnership); but all these recent buildings seem to him to provide strong evidence of a new awareness of style, which is essential when working in contexts such as Miami Beach, Coral Gables, and Coconut Grove.

This book, initiated in Europe, should be seen not as a comprehensive survey of the architecture of Miami today, but as another viewpoint on the city — the viewpoint of dazzled Europeans, transfixed by the beauty, the poetry, the people, and the life they have discovered there.

The point of this publication is not so much to present unknown, hitherto unseen works, as to bring together and define the relationships between architectures that are for the most part already familiar to the people of Miami. The authors hope that the choice and arrangement of images, together with the rhythm of the script, will create the necessary alchemy, and that the imaginations of American and European readers will in turn be set on fire under the tropical sun.

Lobby of the Shelborne Hotel.
Arch: Igor Polevitsky, 1941.
© Historical Association of Southern Florida, (photo: Ernest Graham, 1941).

Shelborne Hotel.
Arch: Igor Polevitsky, 1941.
© Steven Brooke.

This book is therefore not a balance sheet and an end in itself. Its reason for being and its future lie in its impact, in the curiosity it hopes to arouse, and in the other works and exhibitions that may result from it.

Having reached the end of this mosaic of memories, of varied impressions, of things seen and read, of information received, my feeling is that Miami reveals itself only to drifters: if you approach the city with no preconceived ideas or plans, then things, people, places, and events will come to you as if by magic, in the Magic City.

1. Marjory Stoneman Douglas, *The Everglades, River of Grass*, illustrated by Robert Fink. Hurricane House Publishers, Coconut Grove, Florida, ninth edition (first edition 1947).

2. All numbers relate to 1988 datas. There are 75,000 Colombians; 36,000 Salvadorians; 28,000 Puertoricans; 21,000 Dominicans; 19,000 Hondurans; 10,000 Mexicans and 6,000 Chileans.

3. See on this subject: Joaquim Roy, *The Streets of Coral Gables, their names and meanings*, Idea 92 Publications, University of Miami, 1989 — the first of a series of works on relations between Spain and the United States.

4. This hotel has had a troubled history, as told by Helen Muir in *The Biltmore, Beacon for Miami*, Pickering Press, 1987. The hotel closed in 1980 due to financial difficulties. At the fine of writing, it is scheduled to reopen in 1983.

5. These quotations are taken from the book by Donald W. Curl, *Mizner's Florida*, MIT Press, 1989.

6. The most active and influential practices in Miami since the 1950s include, roughly in their order of founding: Pancoast, Ferendino, Grafton, Spillis, & Candela, the most prestigious firm in Miami, founded in the 1940s and still active; Steward & Skinner; Smith, Korach, Hayet, & Haynie; Weed, Russell, & Johnson: Jamison, Nims, & Kruse; Robert M. Little & Associates; J. Wahl & Snyder & Associates; Herbert H. Johnson & Associates; Forfar & Abele; Severuud, Knight, Boerema, & Buff; Ferguson, Glasgow, & Schuster; Bouterse, Perez, & Fabregas. The latter practice was between 1975 and 1985 a leading exponent of the romantic Modernist trend (of which Charles H. Pawley is almost the only representative today). And along with Barbara Capitman, it played an important part in preserving the Art Deco District of Miami Beach South, securing the restoration of several buildings. None of these practices, however, have had as much impact on the Miami skyline in the last few years as Arquitectonica. In 1980, Andres Duany & Elizabeth Plater-Zyberk created the most influential practice concerned with community-orientated urban planning and helped regain for architects some of the authority in public spaces and urban art they had lost to traffic engineers.

"Arrow" in the Tropics.
Rosario Marquardt, oil on paper, 1987.

Collection Luisa & René Murai © Rosario Marquardt.

THE THREE TRADITIONS OF MIAMI

ANDRES DUANY &
ELIZABETH PLATER-ZYBERK

The Cracker vernacular: the Barnacle
(circa 1892). Coconut Grove.
© *Historical Association of Southern Florida.*

Miami is a young city. It has been about a hundred years since its settlement and less than seventy years since it began to have the most minimal urban presence. There has not been time to complicate matters and, without doing violence to reality, one can say that there are only three architectural traditions: the simple wooden vernacular of the first forty years, called Cracker after the pioneers; the sophisticated and abused Mediterranean Revival of the 20s; and that peculiar brand of frivolous Modernism which began in Miami Beach in the 30s, followed in the Brasilia style of the 50s through the hands of Morris Lapidus, and which is now spectacularly in the care of Arquitectonica.

The traditions emerged sequentially, but they did not entirely replace each other. The three now coexist. The thinking architects of Miami continue to work within one or another of these traditions and to defend the virtues of their preference as the only appropriate architecture for the place.

Each can make a strong case. The Cracker vernacular, employed by the first settlers of the state who were known for their simple agricultural ways, holds the high moral ground in every way. It has the honor of primacy. It has the virtue of being an austere architectural language derived from the straightforward expression of construction and materials. It is a light-weight wood architecture abundantly equipped with overhangs for rains and porches for breeze, and so is the best for the hot humid climate.

The contemporary Cracker tradition: the Adler House.
Arch: Rufus Nims, 1952.
Ezra Stoller © Esto.

The contemporary Cracker tradition:
the Collins residence.
Coconut Grove.
Arch: Peter Jefferson, 1961.
© Peter Jefferson.

This architecture was compelling in the 50s and 60s to the idealistically educated architects, but it is deficient in three ways which are important to the current generation.

The first is specific to the world of inexpensive speculative building, which is Miami's primary industry: it is too demanding in craftsmanship. Wood construction requires a degree of precision in the assemblage of its parts which does not exist in the building industry in Miami. The second is that it does not have within its typological repertoire a capability for real urbanism. Individual porches can be aligned on streets, and fences can successfully define public spaces, but when it comes to a real downtown, it can hardly deliver. This is a shortfall for architects for whom urbanism is the discipline of architecture. Thirdly, and admittedly a self-indulgence, this architecture with so short a tradition cannot keep an academically inclined architect interested for a lifetime: a year or two of passionate study, and all the great buildings are known and there is nothing new.

The second tradition, the Mediterranean Revival, which followed in the 10s and 20s, more than compensates for the Cracker's deficiencies. The Mediterranean Revival represents a period of American architecture which looked to exotic sources for its inspiration. A composite translation of vernacular and high classical models taken from all sides of the Mediterranean, this style is most prevalent in Florida and California, although examples exist throught out the United States. It is heir to the vast tradition of Antiquity and of the Renaissance, of the cities of Italy, Spain, and its former colonies of Latin America, but also to specific masters: Palladio, Schinkel, Wagner, Loos, Asplund and the young Aalto. It includes the High Game of Edwin Lutyens, which is enough for a lifetime of discovery and challenge.

Urbanistically, it is not necessary to extoll the extraordinary quality and versatility of the Mediterranean tradition. The architects of the 20s left us brilliant examples in Florida. Furthermore, its masonry and stucco construction is capable of sustaining, not to say revelling in, mediocre workmanship. This is due to a historical circumstance which is uniquely North American: at the time that our architects discovered Spain and Latin America as a source, these places

The urban versatility of the Mediterranean Revival: the city gate Douglas Entrance. Coral Gables. Arch: Phineas Paist, Walter De Garmo, 1926. Restoration: Villis Candela & Partners.
Dan Forer.

The Mediterranean Revival: the Vizcaya Farm Village. Miami.
© Xavier Iglesias.

The contemporary Mediterranean tradition:
Vilanova House.
Key Biscayne.
Arch: Andres Duany
& Elizabeth Plater-Zyberk,
1983.
© Steven Brooke.

The romantic decrepitude of the
Mediterranean Revival:
house (circa 1920s). Miami.
© Duany & Plater-Zyberk.

had been in economic decline for centuries; so the Mediterranean "style" was brought home with a component of romantic decrepitude, which has proven well adapted to our local primitive building culture.

Climatically, the masonry buildings with thick walls and small openings might not be the best for natural ventilation, but they are protective of excessive sunlight and are superb for air conditioning which is, in any case, the real climate of Miami now.

For those who continue to have the "archaic" habit of enjoying the fresh air, certain elements of Mediterranean architecture, like the loggia, the courtyard, and the tower cannot be done without. Early examples of Mediterranean architecture include the 1916 estate of James Deering, Vizcaya, which literally transplanted pieces of Southern European architecture to Miami, and the numerous scenographically composed buildings such as the Coral Gables Douglas Entrance, the Old City Hall in Miami Beach, and the Freedom Tower in Downtown Miami.

In present-day Miami, an undisciplined Post-Modernism is commonly grafted onto the Mediterranean tradition, causing great damage to its reputation.

The Mediterraneans are viewed as hopelessly degenerate and self-indulgent by the Calvinist crackers, and hopelessly timid and retardataire by the glamorous Modernists. And yet any architect who has worked within this sophisticated tradition cannot possibly simulate the charming ignorance of the Crackers, nor the militant amnesia of the Modernists.

The third tradition, the Modernist, also manages to hold a portion of the high moral ground. This miraculous achievement is possible only in the current intellectual climate. In the manner of *Miami Vice* on television, it achieves magnificent images from the moving automobile, and relies on the convenient storage thereof. The public places, when they exist, are only the private lobbies of condominium buildings and the shopping centre plazas. Yet the Modernists monopolize the holy prerogatives of creativity and the spirit of the time. While one may know better, there is something solid about the tradition of Miami Modernism, otherwise this architecture would not be so compelling.

Frivolous Modernism : the Fountainebleau Hotel. Miami Beach. Arch: Morris Lapidus, 1952.
© Xavier Iglesias.

The Modernist Tradition:
the Imperial Apartments. Miami.
Arch: Arquitectonica International, 1979-1983.

© Steven Brooke.

Frivolous Modernism :
Lincoln Road Mall. Miami Beach.
Arch: Morris Lapidus, 1957.

© Xavier Iglesias.

Frivolous Modernism :
the Bacardi Imports
Headquarters Building.
Miami.
Arch: Enrique Gutierrez,
Sacmag International
(Puerto-Rico), 1963.
Huge *azulejos* cover
the north and south
walls of the tower.
These blue and white
ceramic tile murals,
composed of some
28,000 pieces, were
painted by hand
by artist
Francisco Brennand
in his workshop
in Recife, Brazil.
© *Roland I. Unruh*

A Modernist + Cracker hybrid: Cocoplum House. Coral Gables.
Arch: Andres Duany & Elizabeth Plater-Zyberk, 1991.
© *Sharon Socol.*

A Mediterranean + Modernist hybrid:
Fort-Brescia/Spear House.
Coconut Grove.
Arch: Arquitectonica International, 1990.
© *Xavier Iglesias.*

A Mediterranean + Cracker hybrid:
Tigertail House.
Coconut Grove.
Arch: Mari Tere, Jorge & Luis Trelles.
© *Xavier Iglesias.*

The Modernist arguments are strong. It is an architecture that appears to be indigenous to Miami. It isn't of course, but the real spawning grounds in post-revolution Moscow and the playgrounds of Latin America rarely had sufficient wealth to execute the spectacular frivolities of this brand of Modernism. With the help of the media, it is now the export image of Miami, although the reality is that of a hard-working, productive city of immigrants, not a glamorous product.

Art Deco and tropical Modernism were the dominant styles of the Miami Beach boom. The hotels and apartment houses of the 30s betray their architects' infatuation with the new age, as well as their Beaux-Arts training.

Perhaps, because of its genesis via Latin America, this tradition has none of the sanctimonious, socially conscious, constructionally honest restraints which so dulls Modernism usually in the eye of the American public. Unhampered, it is fantastic and radical and a much-needed leavening for the other two traditions which are conservative through and through. The masters of the Cracker and the Mediterranean have little instinct for the astonishing, only for the amusing, little taste for the radical, only for the correct.

All three architectures of Miami have their strengths, and that is why there are no converts. The architects debate and argue, but no one of consequence has really gone over to another side. Perhaps the challenge of a truly regional architecture is to hybridize the strengths of all three traditions. The difficulty arises in the breeding of the three seamlessly without creating monsters of eclecticism. Some recent attempts have been made to confront the beast. We await the result of this gene-splicing without anxiety; for better or worse, the tropical landscape will swallow all.

A hybrid of the three traditions: a house in Santo Domingo, Dominican Republic.

DREAMS OF CITIES

JEAN-FRANÇOIS LEJEUNE

Construction of the forts by the Floridians.
Les Grands Voyages de Théodore de Bry,
1591. Plate XXX.

© Bibliothèque du Service Historique de la Marine, Château de Vincennes.

Miami from Landsat 5. The North-South distance of the Greater Miami area is approximately 34 miles.
One can see:
– to the north: Hialeah, the industrial and working-class districts;
– in the centre from east to west: Miami Beach, Downtown Miami, Little Havana, International Airport;
– to the south: U.S.1, the suburban expansions, Homestead and the US Air Force base;
– to the west: the edge of the Everglades and the agricultural areas.

© Satellite Maps Inc.,1988.
Image Enhancement by KRS Remote Sensing;
Landsat Data Distributed by the Earth Observation Satellite Company.

Faced with a choice — paradise or apocalypse — one cannot be other than optimistic. As an architect and as a citizen, one can only choose paradise and believe that America does once again anticipate an urban architecture. Creating a new architecture will be neither quick or easy. Nor will it be the same as that required in Europe, for our towns and cities are different. On the other hand, we can no longer feign youth and naïveté *as an excuse, nor should we. If the circumstances of our birth gave us an insufficient urban language, then we have the power and the knowledge to expand it. Indeed, we have the responsibility to do so.*[1]

No lands were more hostile to the colonizing efforts of the Conquistadores during the 16th century — Juan Ponce de Léon, Hernando De Soto, Pedro Ménendez de Avilés — than the coasts of South Florida. The stalwart resistance of the Indians, the ominous presence of the impenetrable Everglades and the treacherous climate ruled out the ambitions and the dreams of the Spanish Crown. Their scattered attempts at establishing a camp near the Indian village of Tequesta at the mouth of the Miami River in Biscayne Bay vanished in the footnotes of history.

Time and again, I have asked myself the same question about the origins of Miami. From the standpoint of urban history, was Miami so unfortunate not to have been founded by the Spaniards, on the pattern of thousands of cities in the Caribbean and in South America. Following the *Ordinances for the Discovery, the Population and the Pacification of the Indies,*[2] a section of the "Laws of the Indies" edicted by Philip II of Spain in 1573, they would have laid out the new city on a regular gridiron plan, with narrow streets protected from the sun, and at its heart the main public space, the *plaza mayor.* Of ample dimensions and lined with arcades, the square *plaza* would have opened onto the waters of Biscayne Bay, like Havana's *Plaza de Armas* or the central squares of Campeche and Vera Cruz on the Caribbean coast of Mexico.

At the pioneer Julia Tuttle's invitation, Henri Flagler arrived in Miami in 1896. The railroad tycoon hastily designed the city on a rectangular grid; but as the centrepiece of its plan, he didn't reserve the square, which Miami misses so much, but built the symbol of the city of leisure, the Royal Palm Hotel and its gardens — destroyed in the early 30s and since used as a parking lot — on the most beautiful site at the intersection of the river and the Bay. By a stroke of fortune, a coastal avenue appeared on the early plan, the future Biscayne Boulevard. But the property owners of the Coconut Grove Trail, laired in their tropical landscape, and the profit-driven developers of the northern sections along the bay failed to prolong Flagler's vision and eliminated all public access to the water. By doing so, they miserably missed the opportunity to build the grand coastal boulevard, rival of the *malecons* of Havana, Cartagena and other Caribbean cities, and allowed their neighbors in Tampa and West Palm Beach to boast of their long seashore drives. The same situation prevailed in Miami Beach where bay and ocean frontages were entirely privatized, with the exception of the ten blocks of Ocean Drive at the heart of the Deco District.

Despite these mishaps, many other scandals and embezzlements — humorously narrated in John Rothchild's classic *Up for Grabs* — the first decades of the city did not lack optimistic times and flashes of visionary imagination.[3]

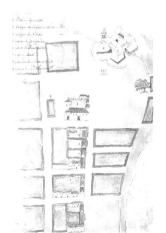

Plan of the Plaza
de Armas in Havana with
the Parish Church and the
Fort of La Fuerza, 1691.
Archivo General de Indias,
M. y P. Santo Domingo, 96.
© *Archivo General de Indias, Seville.*

"The Mediterranean, the Caribbean and the Gulf of Mexico form a homogeneous though interrupted sea" wrote A.J. Liebling, in his novel *The Earl of Louisiana.*[4] In 1916, the architects of Villa Vizcaya, Francis Burrall Hoffmann and Paul Chalfin, shook off the "tropical Far West" rags of Miami: the Venitian connection was born — "*le mythe de Venise dans Miami désert,*"[5] the "analogous" Venice in the words of Aldo Rossi, that of the Venetian Islands, the Venetian pool and the contemporary Ca' Ziff:

While you regard the silent palace, mirroring the whiteness of its walls, towers, and terraces in the clear water, as a Venetian palace would be mirrored in the lagoon, it is not difficult to imagine a Longhi figure, clad in somber drapery, descending stone steps and embarking towards the Keys; and if, in the distance, the tall and slender silhouette of a campanile should stand against the sky, the illusion of the Venetian "lidi" would be completed.[6]

In the booming 1920s, the Spanish world and its American offspring — the novels of Washington Irving and the Pan-American expositions of San Diego and San Francisco — inspired and nurtured new "dreams of cities:" the three campaniles, built by the New York giants Schultze and Weaver, replicas of Seville's *Giralda*; Carl Fisher's resort of Miami Beach; Hialeah and Opa-Locka, the ideal cities conceived by the aviator Glenn Curtiss; and the most important American garden city, Coral Gables and its thousands of "Castles in Spain" by the developer-poet-urbanist George Merrick. Of all these founders, Merrick was apparently the only one to embrace a metropolitan vision of the future big city, a genuine Pan-American metropolis at the meeting place of North and South. "The tourist of today will be the Miamian of Tomorrow," he wrote in his pamphlet *The Romance of Real Estate*. In 1937, almost ten years after his eviction from Coral Gables government, Merrick — the solitary voice of a modern Cassandra — was still urging the future planning of a greater Miami, and continued to promote his democratic dreams of new parks and public spaces: the International Park of Flowers, the Tropical Gardens — and of a fifty-mile long bayside boulevard Beira Mar encircling Biscayne Bay.

But now we are not only visioning a big city, but a great city, one truly great! Such a city is balanced. Such a city is of proportion. Such balance, and such proportion as are so satisfying as one looks at some of these old ancient Colonial homes of New England, proper balance, proper proportion. And it is in such a truly great city and only in such, that we may have individually and collectively a future of greatest satisfaction and of greatest

Skyline of Miami at night.
Postcard.
© Historical Association of Southern Florida.

prosperity. Our great city of balance and proportion must have water access for all our residents, whether Bay-fronters or ten miles back from the Bay. Thus the Coconut Grove Trail of the yesterdays will be transformed into the 50 mile loop, that can similarly be used by all of us for selling and for satisfying the million.[7]

Until 1959, Miami remained a provincial city, a Key West-like vacation place, barely disturbed by the first skyscrapers, the search lights of Biscayne Boulevard, and the city-like hotels of Morris Lapidus on Collins Avenue. It was Castro's revolution in Cuba which would eventually trigger the metamorphosis of the city. In three decades, Miami has become the unexpected capital of the Caribbean, a gigantic "Ellis Island," more or less clandestine, whose symbol has long been the former *Miami Daily News* campanile, facing the Bay and renamed "Freedom Tower."

Refuge of all those fleeing dictatorships, but also of the fleeing dictators, Greater Miami is now an ironic version of the metropolis envisioned by George Merrick: two million residents and more than two million vehicles bustle briskly, in a permanent Brownian movement, in a narrow strip of land, thirty-five miles long, between the Gulf Stream, the Atlantic Ocean and the inviolable frontier of what has been spared of the Everglades.

THE AIRPLANE AND THE GARDEN CITIES

The architect and urbanist Le Corbusier never worked in Miami, but a quick aerial sketch of the city could make us believe that his plans for Rio de Janeiro or Buenos Aires had been realized in the subtropical landscape — except for the fact that the highrises and the elevated freeways overlook an ocean of houses sprawling on a limitless grid. Seaplanes, airplanes and other identified flying objects have always completed the city and its skyline. Hence, it is from the air that Miami — the "truly contemporary city," the "city without qualities" to paraphrase Musil — unveils the conflicting visions of beauty and absurdity. For there

Vault of banyans on
Columbus Avenue,
Coral Gables.
© Jean-François Lejeune.

is the beauty of the "seaside" and "garden" cities, too often violently conquering an inhospitable nature — Biscayne Bay and its artificial islands, the grand hotels along the miles of beaches and canals, the courtyards of South Beach — the fascinating but incomplete adaptation of Tony Garnier's *Cité Industrielle* to

Airplanes flying over
Biscayne Bay.
Postcard.
© Historical Association of Southern
Florida.

The Fitzgerald Apartments. 15th Street, Miami Beach.
Arch: Henry Hohauser, 1939.
© Th. Delbeck & M. Tedeskino.

Marlin Hotel. Washington Avenue, Miami Beach.
Arch: L. Murray Dixon, 1939.
© Jean-François Lejeune.

Ocean Drive, Miami Beach (before widening of the sidewalks).
© Th. Delbeck & M. Tedeskino.

Alinn Apartments. Pennsylvania Avenue, Miami Beach. 1937.
Arch: Henry J. Maloney, 1937.
© Jean-François Lejeune.

The metromover in
Downtown Miami.
© Rogier Van Eck.

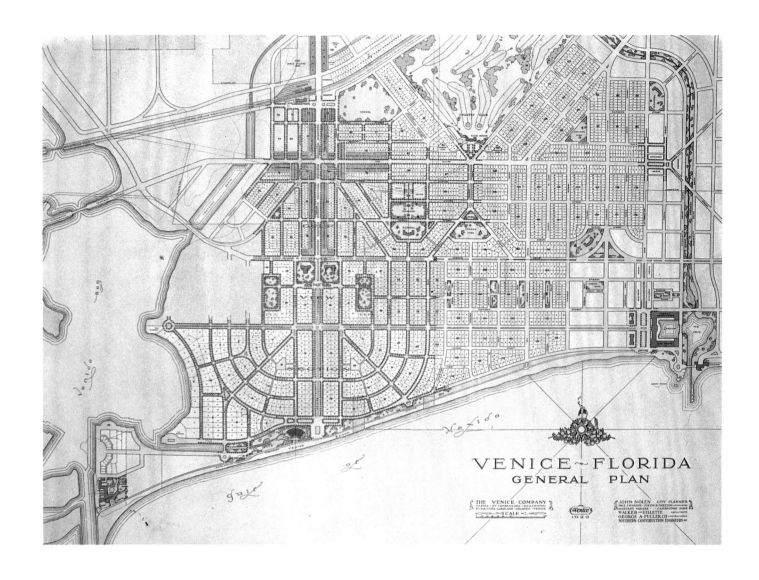

Venice, General Plan, 1926.
The new town of Venice
on the West Coast of Florida
during the Florida boom of the 1920s.
John Nolen planned more than
twenty new towns and villages.
Many of them, like Venice,
have been a successful developments.

© John Nolen Research Fund and Papers, Cornell University Libraries.

the early tourism industry,[8] the "architecture of the trees" defining the jungle-like streets of Coconut Grove and the green vaults of Coral Gables — literal transcriptions of the *Scena Satirica* in Sebastiano Serlio's *Second Book of Architecture (1541)*. There are the royal palm colonnades of the Deering Estate, of the Hialeah Race Track, and of the Fairchild Tropical Gardens. There are the skyscrapers, the metrorail and the splendor of the city at night...

In the 1920s, the urbanist John Nolen talked about Florida as "the great urban laboratory" where "new towns should express new standards and new ideals, and be an attempt to meet in new ways the modern conditions of life."[9] Today, from the busy skies of South Florida, "THE AIRPLANE INDICTS"[10] generations of architects, planners, bureaucrats and politicians who have transformed this Garden of Eden into a national laboratory of physical fragmentation, social isolation and urban de-construction. There is Downtown, uninhabited and soulless at night, the absurd zoning codes enslaving residents to the automobile, the limitless growth of the suburbs paving over the Everglades and the agricultural lands, the miles of shopping centres chaotically aligned along the oversized highways, the thousands of acres of cocooned subdivisions, walled and often guarded, in search of absolute intimacy and safety... There in a fury of picturesque, anti-Beaux-Arts and anti-modern urbanism, the grid of streets — the last legacy of American urbanity — has vanished under the bulldozers of megalomaniac engineers and the advocates of the "safe" cul-de-sacs.

In the mid-1980s, along a beach on the Gulf of Mexico, the new town of Seaside emerged from this nightmare as the innocent urban archetype, the mythical town of childhood carved out of an oak forest like a modern Savannah, the American version of the Proustian memories of *A la Recherche du Temps Perdu*.
All of a sudden, the small town became a cult icon, a media star spawning an unprecedented wave of interest in architecture and townplanning: journals and books on architecture, *Time* and *Newsweek*, fashion magazines, and the Prince

of Wales's film *A Vision for Britain* created the architectural event of the decade. The founding of the town, the actors and the milestones of its short history, already belong to urban legend : Robert Davis, the founder and developer, former political activist of Miami; his team of architects, Andres Duany, a Cuban

In the 70s, the developer and founder of Seaside, Robert Davis (and Daryl) traveling the American South in search of the vernacular types.
© *Robert Davis.*

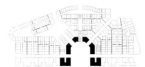

Type I. Central square.

Type 2. *Vieux Carré*,
New Orleans.

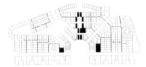

Type 3. Townhouses.

Type 4. "Antebellum" houses.

PLAN OF THE NEW TOWN OF
SEASIDE, FLORIDA - 1990

Direction: Jean-Francois LeJeune,
Frank Martinez.
Team: Luay Al-Saleh, Ana Alvarez,
Juan Calvo, Virginia Del Rosal,
Laura Garofalo, Christine Gradie,
Christine Lopez, Jihad Mikati.
In the post-war suburbs,
the urban conventions
of the lot and the block were lost,
resulting in the lack of any real

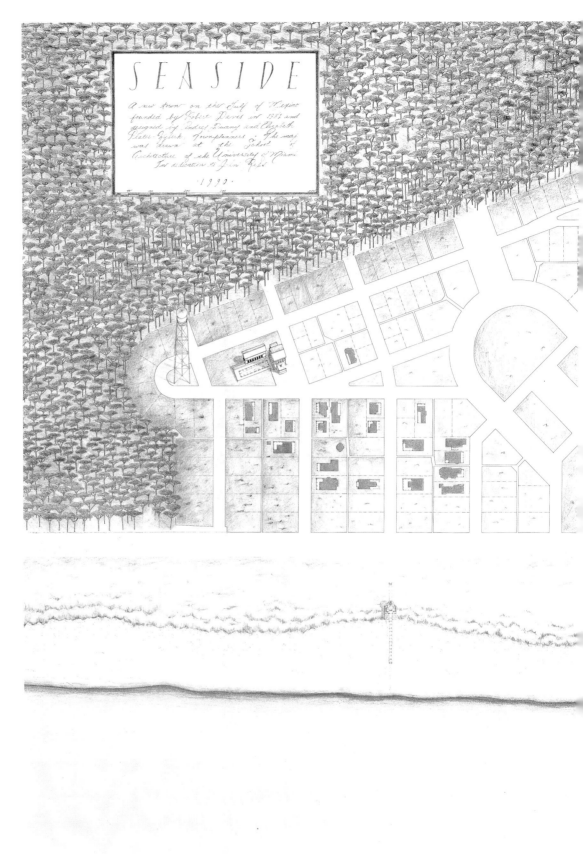

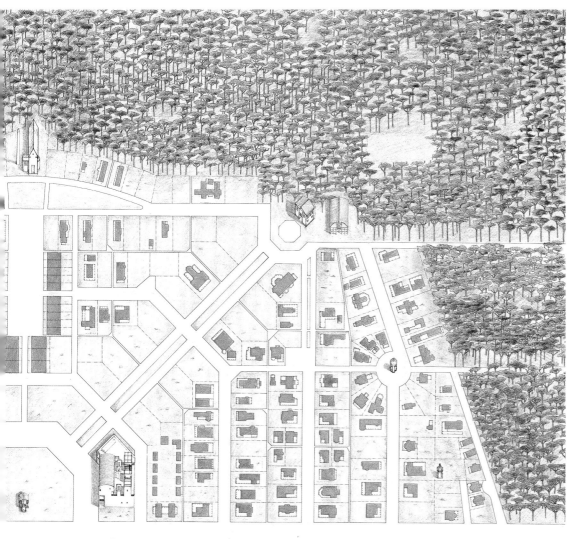

Type 5. Special groupings.

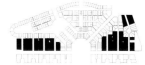

Type 6. Detached cottages.

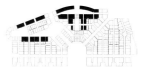

Type 7. "Charleston" houses.

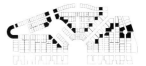

Type 8. Detached cottages.

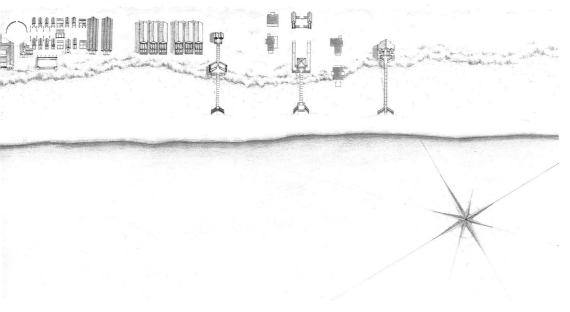

public space. Seaside marks the
return to the traditional planning,
with the division of the land.
into lots, built by owners and
small developers.
The lots have a standard width,
varying from 25 to 65 feet.
The average depth is 100 feet.
The dimensions and proportions
of the lots are specifically related
to their intended use and the type
of public space they shape.

© University of Miami School of Architecture

of the "exile" generation, and Elizabeth Plater-Zyberk, an American of Polish parents, cofounders of Arquitectonica which they left to create their own firm in 1980;[11] driving in a convertible across the Deep South in search of the ideal town; the masterplan finalized between 1978 and 1981 in a shotgun house shipped to the site from a neighboring town[12]; the advice of the London architect and urbanist Leon Krier, who later built his first work, a temple-house overlooking the city; the intimate streets and the footpaths nicknamed the *Krierwalks*; the wooden houses and their traditional front porches tending to talk; the white neo-classical post office designed by Davis himself; the pavilions, sentinels on the beach; the grey concrete of the Hybrid Building anchored by Steven Holl on the central square, and whose arcades shade souvenir shops and ice-cream parlors...

Beyond its nostalgic image, Seaside should be interpreted as an urban laboratory or, more audaciously, as an exhibition city, comparable at the end of the 20th century to the *1893 Columbian Exposition of Chicago*, i.e., in a moment of dramatic urban crisis, a catalyst against anarchic growth, a window for a new urbanism.

Indeed, under the leadership of Daniel Burnham, the "White City" was the starting point of the *City Beautiful Movement*. Whereas its grandiose visions of regional planning and embellishment of the urban centres — epitomized, among others, in the Plan of Chicago (1908) and the plan for Washington — were inspired by Paris and the Beaux-Arts methods of composition, it was the more modest objective of reestablishing the principles of the American urbanity that Duany and Plater-Zyberk assigned to the small Floridian town.

Undoubtedly, the commercial and intellectual success of Seaside is the irrational result of a very rational process:

Seaside is the accomplished formulation of an "impossible dream" (except in its commercial version of Disneyworld) which has been haunting, whether consciously or not, Americans confronted by the isolation: the growing social costs of suburbanization: the longing for the recuperation of both the lost public realm and the patriotic values epitomized in the semi-urban landscape of the small town and of the most admired urban neighborhoods

Rosewalk cottages.
Arch: Robert Orr
and Melanie Taylor.
© Th. Delbeck and M Tedeskino.

With the central square or "green," Main Street, lined with shops, public buildings and monuments, and the Arcadian treelined residential streets, the small town is for Duany and Plater-Zyberk the American version of the French village or the Italian hill town. Similarly, the best neighborhoods of American cities such as Savannah, Charleston, Key West, Asheville, New Orleans or Williamsburg represent ideal models for urban living quite different from their European counterparts. The ubiquitous grid pattern of streets, excessively criticized by the writers of American urban history, is no longer interpreted as a diabolic invention of greedy developers but as a rational urban system, a necessary condition of American urbanity, even though it has been generally used in the most elementary fashion. In reexamining these sources in the design of Seaside, Duany and Plater-Zyberk have succeeded in redeeming the contradictory visions of the small town — an ideal of community and human balance, but also a synonym of boredom and economic stagnation. In doing so, they have metamorphosed the image of the small town — urban Janus in the films of Robert Capra, Steven Spielberg and David Lynch — into a model for the end-of-the-century community, a substantial alternative to the segregation and monofunctional organization of the postwar suburbs.

Seaside, together with the projects that have followed, is not a traditional American town but its reinvention. Its plan is an intellectual exercise, a unique and hybrid synthesis of the major guiding concepts in the history of American urbanism: the Jeffersonian grid, the formalism of the *City Beautiful Movement* and the scenographic effects borrowed from the garden city movement and the theories of Camillo Sitte and Raymond Unwin. The wealth and diversity of typologies — the detached house, the arcaded building, the townhouse, the "Charleston" house — and their unusual ordering, suggest a comparison with the experiment of the *Case Study Houses* in Los Angeles. The result of this competition, launched in 1945 by the *Arts and Architecture* magazine, was a series of prototype houses, built between 1945 and 1961, which have defined the paradigm of "the Californian dream."

Seaside is a similar but ideologically antithetical attempt. For its houses do not exhibit significant stylistic and constructive changes, but more importantly the reestablishment of the traditional relationship between

Pool Pavilion.
Arch: Derrick Smith.
© *Delbeck & Tedeschino.*

house and street. The return of the "front porch," a symbolic feature of the American house ousted after the War by the two-car garage door, is an example among others.

The critic who would equate Seaside with François Spoerry's Port Grimaud near St-Tropez or William Ellis' Portmeirion in the Wales would be mistaken. Seaside has not been an isolated experiment but the harbinger of an urbanistic debate and movement which has been spreading across the United States. Like Daniel Burnham in the heyday of the *City Beautiful*, Andres Duany and Elizabeth Plater-Zyberk have been invited to lecture and to work from coast to coast. More than thirty projects are in progress: new suburban neighborhoods designed as small towns, such as the Kentlands and Belmont near Washington; small resort villages like Windsor, Florida and Tannin, Alabama; redevelopment plans for inner-city neighborhoods in Trenton, New Jersey, and St Louis, Missouri; and ambitious "new towns" like Wellington and Avalon in Florida, both covering more than 5,000 acres. Paradoxically, it is in Los Angeles that, in collaboration with Stefanos Polyzoïdes and Elizabeth Moule, they have designed their most urban projects: a Downtown masterplan in the wake of the 1992 riots and, on the 750 acres of the former Howard Hughes airport south of Venice, a new mixed-use neighborhood. This project is articulated on a dense grid of blocks, streets and squares and on a structure of boulevards planted with tall palm trees in the great scenographic tradition of Beverly Hills, Santa Monica and Pasadena.

In view of their urban form and their typological characteristics, these plans are the forerunners of a new generation of garden cities. Indeed, following on Robert Stern's writings,[13] Duany and Plater-Zyberk believe that, in the writing of the history of 20th-century architecture, the Anglo-American suburbs have been overlooked or ignored as potential models. In Coral Gables as well as in the works of Unwin, Nolen, Brunner, Kessler, etc., they have identified the sophisticated

Avalon Park.
Central Florida, 1990.
Town planners:
Andres Duany &
Elizabeth Plater-Zyberk.
Sketch of a
neighborhood square.
Drawing: Charles Barrett.
© Andres Duany & Elizabeth Plater-Zyberk.

solutions and the beginnings of a theory of a New City born with the automobile and adapted to its use. Two organizational principles distinguish this new generation: first, the division into neighborhoods whose size is based upon a five to ten minute walking distance; second, the taking into account of

Aerial view of a neighborhood.
Design: Jorge Hernandez and Jean-François Lejeune.
© Andres Duany & Elizabeth Plater-Zyberk.

NEW TOWN OF WELLINGTON
Palm Beach, 1990
Town planners: Andres Duany & Elizabeth Plater-Zyberk

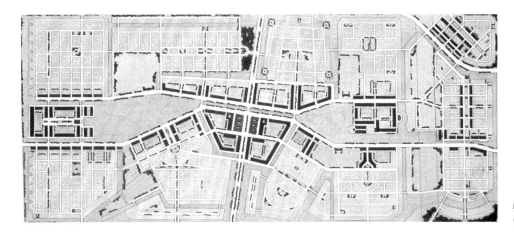

Masterplan.
© Andres Duany & Elizabeth Plater-Zyberk.

parking requirements as a necessary module for the dimensioning of blocks and lots. The attractiveness of these garden cities, for the professional as for the public, rests on simple design solutions: patterns of streets, avenues and squares generally continuous and based on the grid and its variations, a limited number of party wall buildings spatially defining streets and squares of neighborhood centres, detached houses along Elm streets and back alleys, large planted squares designed to accommodate parking in the expectation that a revolution could return them to the pedestrians... As for the public buildings and monuments, they mirror the reality of modern life — schools, churches, meeting halls, clubhouses, and in some cases city halls, theatres and universities — and are all fully interwoven into the plan.

The reinvention of the American garden city at the time of the sprawling metropolis is a sign of postmodernism. It is no longer conceived within the utopian and Jeffersonian vision of a production unit linked to craft and agricultural production, but is inherently dependent on the service economy and computer networks. Like Ebenezer Howard, the Miami urbanists do not partake in an agrarian, anti-urban, "back to the country" nostalgia. Since it attempts to solve the problems of urban expansion rather than fight them, their work is fundamentally urban. In 1945, Lewis Mumford wrote in his preface to the new edition of *Garden Cities of Tomorrow*: "The garden city, in the manner defined by Howard, is not a mere green suburb, but its antithesis: not a banal rural retreat, but a complex creation for an effective urban life."[14]

THE SCHOOL OF MIAMI AND THE NEW URBANISM

In the action line of American pragmatism, Duany and Plater-Zyberk have soon acknowledged that the war against suburban mediocrity must be waged in the trenches of private development, the unavoidable reality of urban and profit-driven growth. Applying word for word Le Corbusier's formula recipe "Sound urbanism does not spend money. IT MAKES MONEY,"[15] they dared claim that in the United States "something built is more revolutionary than something drawn." With this language, their professional and media crusade has found new allies among the public, the media, the architects and the public servants. Their work inspires confidence, for it is a long-term alternative to wasted space and energy, to traffic gridlock, and to the environmental pollution that plague the city of

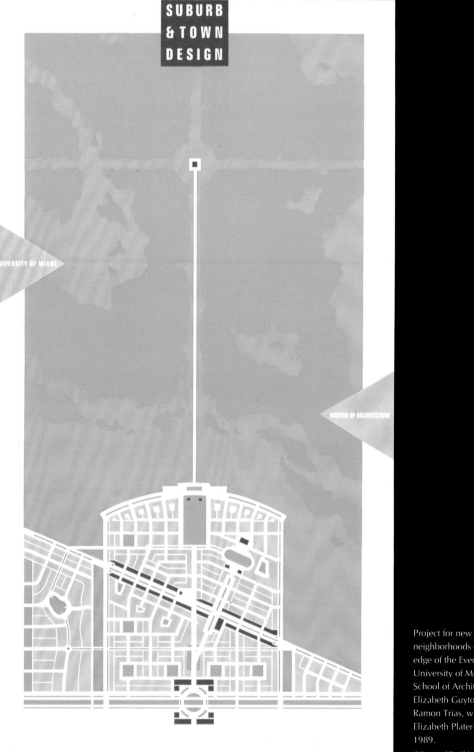

SUBURB & TOWN DESIGN

UNIVERSITY OF MIAMI

MASTER OF ARCHITECTURE

Project for new
neighborhoods on the
edge of the Everglades.
University of Miami
School of Architecture,
Elizabeth Guyton,
Ramon Trias, with
Elizabeth Plater-Zyberk
1989.

© University of Miami School of Architecture

zones. To achieve these aims, the most radical aspect of their work is the concept of urban codes. An unknown but important part of early American history, urban codes guided, among others, the planning of Savannah and of the cities founded according to the "Laws of the Indies," like St Augustine and Santa Fe. Later they contributed to the building of 19th-century Back Bay in Boston, and to the reconstruction of Santa Barbara after the earthquake of 1925. Similarly, the "1916 Zoning Act" of New York generated the landmark skyscrapers. Nowadays, the sprawling suburbs and disintegrating urban centres are neither the products of a *laissez-faire* policy nor the inevitable consequence of heedless greed. Rather, they have been planned as such, the direct result of zoning and subdivision ordinances devoid of any spatial dimension and blindly administered by hundreds of planning departments. Ironically, the regulatory situation is such that architects are being banned from building in the manner of the most admired places in America. In every part of the United States, the construction of a new Williamsburg, Charleston or San Francisco would be virtually forbidden by the existing codes.

In Duany & Plater-Zyberk's masterplans, a graphic urban code monitors the types of buildings and street sections, the distribution of functions, the height of the buildings and their distance from street edges. Contrary to the mere abstractions of current regulations, the urban codes draw from time-honored examples of successful European and American urbanism, not merely to reproduce them but to improve and adapt them to new conditions of life. In Seaside, the extolled urban code — by authorizing some small volumes to go beyond the height limit — has been ultimately responsible for the idiosyncratic skyline topped by wooden towers and belvederes, like a vernacular version of medieval San Gimignano in Italy.

Andres Duany keenly refers to this aspect of their work as revolutionary tactics: "During the Cuban revolution, Castro bought radio transmitters to broadcast the revolution across the island. What we are proposing now is to get hold of the architectural radio transmitters: the codes." With other professionals, they have designed a general urban code applicable to the fifty states. The *Traditional Neighborhood Ordinance* aims at two main objectives: first, to give a legal foundation to neighborhoods and towns integrating all functions in close distance, and second, to help create new "cities of tolerance" allowing all ways of life, without prejudice. Indeed, current zoning codes are not neutral and they have perpetuated social and economic segregation, reducing *de facto* the free-dom to choose one's environment. By liberating the residents from the compul-sory use of the automobile, the *Traditional Neighborhood Ordinance* will eventually lower energy consumption and personal stress.

By stating loudly fifty years after Lewis Mumford that the American Dream has been betrayed and by clearly blaming the culprits, Andres Duany and Elizabeth Plater-Zyberk have unearthed a Pandora's box of frustrations and desertions. At the same time, they have brought some authority and respectability back into the realm of planning and to the devalued profession of urbanist. At the School of Architecture of the University of Miami, they, along with the faculty, have re-stored the design of cities as a full-fledged discipline of architecture and edu-cation.[16]

The theories of the "School of Miami" have gained widespread acceptance. Ricardo Legoretta, Charles Moore and Rodolfo Machado & Jorge Silvetti have been collaborating on some projects; in 1991, Harvard University and Alex Krieger published the first catalogue of their urban work; in California, Stefanos Polyzoïdes & Elizabeth Moule, Peter Calthorpe and Daniel Solomon have found ripe territories for an overhaul of previous urbanistic practices. With the support of international personalities such as the Prince of Wales and Leon Krier, Duany & Plater-Zyberk intend to structure the movement under the name *The New Urbanism*; its First Congress, on the CIAM model, is scheduled for 1993.

The movement aims specifically at lawmakers and public officials confronted with a growing ecologically minded public. Indeed, barring a catastrophe, growth will have to be channeled in revitalized existing neighborhoods and suburbs, and in a limited network of new mixed-use towns and neighborhoods. With provocative zest, Duany and Plater-Zyberk argue that enlightened devel-opers and landowners may be convinced to act as town founders like Nash and Woods in England, Van Scheweringen in Cleveland, Merrick in Coral Gables or David in Seaside. Their thoughts seem to echo Francesco Dal Co whose essay *From Parks to Region* points out how closely related are the concept of the garden city and the American tradition of enlightened enterprise at the begin-ning of the century.[17]

This optimistic call to private developers to help create the new "cities of tomorrow" appears quite venturesome. First, the founding of a town is the most symbolic act of possession of new land; it has been performed by many generations. Only in the current century has the settling of land been more and more severed from the society's mythical, cultural and religious aspirations. How to reunite these components of our culture is one of the nettlesome questions related to the city of the 21st century.

Besides, can the accretion of small towns, each by a separate developer, eventually create a real urbanity unless they are interrelated within a more elaborate urbanistic and political context — in the Greek sense of *polis*? In the absence of such a global project, only a small step separates the "ideal community" from the "tyrannies of intimacy" denounced by Richard Sennett:

The city is the instrument of impersonal life, the mold in which diversity and complexity of persons, interests, and tastes become available as social experience. The fear of impersonality is breaking that mold. In their nice, neat gardens, people speak of the horrors of London or New York; here in Highgate or Scarsdale one knows one's neighbors; true, not much happens, but life is safe. It is retribalization. The terms of "urbane" and "civilized" now connote the rarefied experiences of a small class, and are tinged with the rebuke of snobbism. It is the very fear of impersonal life, the very value put upon intimate contact, which makes the notion of a civilized experience, in which people are comfortable with a diversity of experience, and indeed find nourishment in it, a possibility only for the rich and well-bred. In this sense, the absorption in intimate affairs is the mark of uncivilized society. [18]

CARIBBEAN DREAMS

Will *The New Urbanism*, conceived and nurtured in Miami, affect the future of the city? Has the "large city of unlimited growth" reached its social, energetic and ecological limits? At best, the answer is ambiguous, for the debate on the

Biscayne Boulevard early in the century, before the construction of Bayfront Park into the Bay.
© *Historical Association of Southern Florida.*

future of Greater Miami has remained modest and limited in audience. In the suburbs, the destructive codes continue to prevail, and they now threaten existing urban neighborhoods; traffic engineers pursue their unrelenting task, eventually botching neighborhoods and landscape. In counterpoint, one cannot but praise

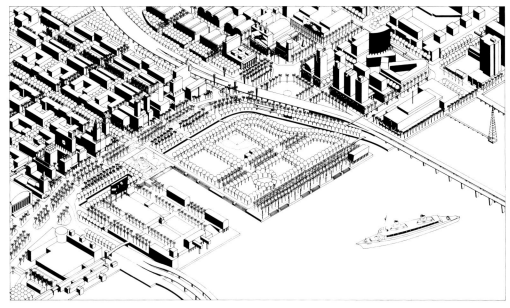

Axonometric view.
Arch: Jean-François Lejeune, with Alan Shulman.

© Jean-François Lejeune · University of Miami · School of Architecture.

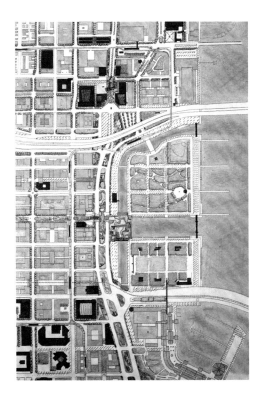

MASTERPLAN FOR BISCAYNE BOULEVARD
DOWNTOWN MIAMI, 1992
Urbanists: Jean-François Lejeune
and Jaime Correa,
with Cesar Garcia-Pons, Raul Lastra, Dana Little

The Masterplan — first studied for the Downtown
Development Authority — proposes a vision for
the future of Dowtown and Biscayne Boulevard.
The project includes the construction of two new
neighborhoods (ParkWest and Omni), the
construction of an Opera Hall and a Symphony
Hall on opposite sides of the boulevard, the
reconstruction of the expressway bridges and the
renovation of the existing parks — the abandoned
FEC tract as a recreational active park with
terminal structures for cruisehips; and
Bicentennial Park as an urban tropical park.

Masterplan
(yellow: housing and other fabric; red: public buildings).

© University of Miami School of Architecture

the efforts to restore Coral Gables, Opa-Locka, Morningside and other neighbor-hoods, the public involvement of citizens' groups, and their battle for public parks. First used as a monumental but empty stage set by Michael Mann in the television series *Miami Vice*, South Beach, has now become — thanks to the early leadership of the late "pioneer" Barbara Capitman — a denser and more demo-cratic version of Seaside, a full-fledged neighborhood and for the second time in ten years the most mediatic urban scene in Florida and in the country. South Beach underscores the thesis of the"School of Miami," it indicates that the time has come for Miami to brush aside the myths of the "American Dream" — those exalted by the movie industry and its European servants Jean Baudrillard and Wim Wenders: the romance of the road, the trailer, the drive-in, the natural and manmade canyons,… On the contrary, the new dreams of cities, discussed and conceived in Miami, speak of true neighborhoods and communities, of pleasant streets, of new public squares and promenades. First and foremost, they speak of a new cultural identity, of the architectural and urbanistic translation of the multi ethnic city of the 21st century. Thus, a "new city" might arise, that would inte-grate the urban "Three Traditions" of the region: the vernacular of "the garden and the grid," the "Mediterranean-Caribbean" traditions of the Spanish colonial city, and the machine-based modern city.

Miami, capital of the Caribbean and crossing place of the Americas? Up to now, one searches in vain through this multi ethnic landscape. Little Havana and Little Haiti bring to mind Robert Venturi and Denise Scott-Brown's assertions of *Learning from Las Vegas:* but the neon signs, the Spanish and Creole sounds, and the folk scenes of *Casablanca* and *Versailles,* are not enough to recollect Havana, San Juan or Rio de Janeiro. In the suburbs, the developers still disguise their stan-dardized products under a fake "Mediterranean" varnish. However, it is obvious — and this book ought to be evidence enough — that signs of change, if not of impatience, have appeared. Along with the artists, a new generation of

Windsor.
The mall planted with palms.
On the right, the first courtyard house.
© Jean-François Lejeune.

architects and urbanists eagerly refuses a complete assimilation in the American *main-stream* and claim their origins and cultural roots, be they Caribbean or Latin American.

One could argue that George Merrick in Coral Gables and Addison Mizner in Palm Beach had pursued the same ambitions;

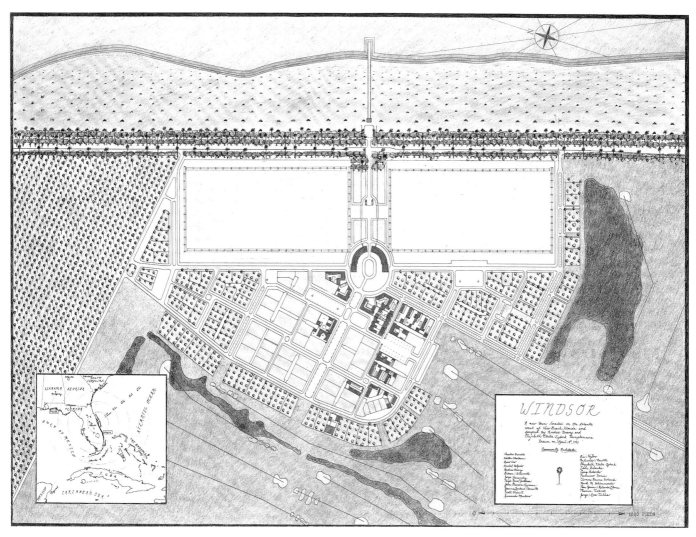

Plan with built and unbuilt houses.
Drawing: Jean-François Lejeune, with Elizabeth Guyton,
Victor Morales, Karen Scheinberg.
© Jean-François Lejeune.

© Jean-François Lejeune.

NEW VILLAGE OF WINDSOR
Vero Beach, 1992
Town planners: Andres Duany & Elisabeth Plater-Zyberk

Aerial view of the village
under construction.
August 1991.
© Windsor, Vero Beach, Florida.

© Windsor, Vero Beach, Florida.

but, their present-day followers don't look at their native cities as mere images to emulate. They intend to use and reproduce their houses, their typologies and their very public spaces. In the absence of such an opportunity in their own city, many Miami architects have stepped into the Windsor showcase. Under construction north of Miami near Vero Beach, the resort village of Windsor proudly advertises its ambition to be an elite product, strictly controlled by Duany and Plater-Zyberk's plans and codes. Its founders have fully accepted the intellectual and commercial challenge of realizing the urban fusion of North and South. The streets of Windsor are narrow, and the walls hide orange groves and gardens. Aligned on the street edge, the houses own, either have a lateral porch and garden as in the Bermudas and Charleston, or a central courtyard as in the colonial quarters of St Augustine, Merida, Maracaibo or Antigua Guatemala. Lined with the largest courtyard houses and two rows of royal palms, the central mall linking the town centre to the golf course has been designed to emulate the grand Spanish colonial *paseos* of Cuba, Colombia, and Puerto-Rico.

Next to Windsor and the other works shown in the chapter "Tropical Cocktail," South Beach may paradoxically be the most tropical district of Miami. Indeed, the white cubical, if not cubist buildings are the only North American realisation of the urban qualities of the "other modern architecture," the one which was to be obliterated by the exclusive northern orientation of the International Style Exhibition in 1932 in New York. This other modern architecture, the southern one, Mediterranean and tropical, is the one that also flourished in Adalberto Libera's and Sabaudia's Rationalist Italy, and in the Casablanca, Tel Aviv and Santiago de Chile of the 1930s.

In 1996, Miami celebrates its centennial. Downtown ought be the stage not of a grand parade, but of the city of the future. While its skyline makes it very "telegenic," Downtown is a caricatural centre, a ghost town for two thirds of its territory, a place unworthy of its natural setting and its international ambitions. Downtown Miami ought to owe its future identity to new "dreams of cities." For the possibility of building a "city within the city" is unique and several projects sustain this vision. At the southern edge of Downtown, the old red-painted Brickell Bridge will be recon-

The Brickell Bridge in 1990.
© Jean François Lejeune.

The old red-painted metal bridge marks the main
entrance to Downtown Miami from the south.
The public outcry against
the reconstruction project by
the Department of Transportation
led the Brickell Bridge Committee to
organize a competition
for an aesthetic architectural
treatment of the
new bridge.

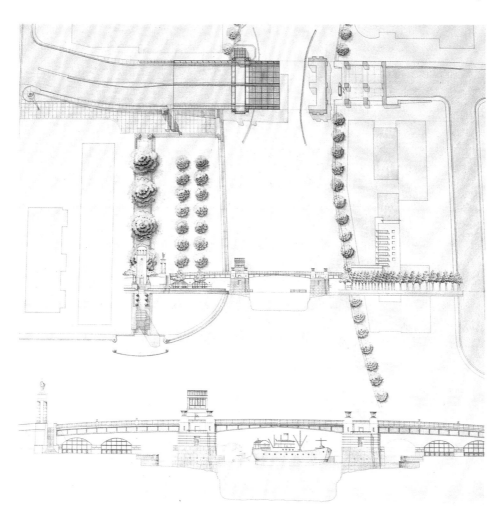

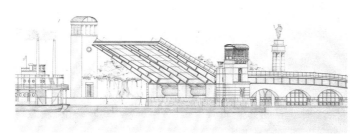

Brickell Bridge Competition .
First Prize.
Arch: Jorge Hernandez,
Rafael Portuondo,
Mike Sardinas.
The project of classical inspiration
will house statues of four historic
figures of Miami: a Tequesta Indian,
Julia Tuttle, Marjory Stoneman
Douglas and Henri Flagler.
© Portuondo-Peratti Architects.

Brickell Bridge Competition.
Arch: Jorge Trelles, Luis Trelles, Mari
Tere Trelles, Joe Valencia.
© Trelles Architects.

Brickell Bridge Competition.
Fifth Prize.
Arch: Roberto M. Béhar,
Teofilo Victoria and
Tomas Lopez-Gottardi.

© Tomas Lopez-Gottardi.

structed as a symbolic gateway to the city. In the prize-winning design reminiscent of Otto Wagner, the piers of the bridge will support statues of four historic Miami figures: a Tequesta Indian, Henry Flagler, Marjory Stoneman Douglas and Julia Tuttle. Immediately to the north, Brazilian landscape architect Roberto Burle-Marx has drawn plans to transform Biscayne Boulevard in a wide tropical and colorful avenue, like Avenida Atlantica along Copacabana Beach that he designed in 1970; a couple of blocks away, the first section of a 120-foot wide *paseo* — later to be extended to Biscayne Boulevard and lined with apartments — was inaugurated in 1992. Along these new public spaces and in this district alone, twenty thousand residents could live a new American way of life, a synthesis of North and South.[19]

Ironically, on the eve of Miami's second and "electronic" century, the two missing monuments of its past remain to be built. The first one must be built in the heart of Downtown: a genuine Miami City Hall, to replace its current and eccentric location at the former Pan American seaplane terminal in Coconut Grove. The second, under discussion for more than ten years, shall be built along Biscayne Boulevard: the grand Symphony and Opera Halls that might finally stop us, citizens of Greater Miami, dreaming of Sidney…

The seaplane Pan American
Terminal in the 1930s, today
the Miami City Hall.
© Historical Association of Southern Florida.

1 Michael Dennis, *Court & Garden, From the French Hôtel to the City of Modern Architecture*, MIT Press, 1986.

2 The text of the "Laws of the Indies" can be found in English and original Spanish in *The New City n⁰ 1, Foundations*, University of Miami School of Architecture, Princeton University Press, pp. 18-33, 1991.

3 John Rothchild, *Up for Grabs: a trip through time and space in the Sunshine*, Viking, New York, 1985.

4 A.J. Liebling, *The Earl of Louisiana*, Simon & Schuster, New York, 1961.

5 The author has taken the liberty of paraphrasing the title of Marguerite Duras' film, *Son nom de Venise dans Calcutta désert*, 1976.

6 Paul Chalfin, "The Gardens of Vizcaya" in *Architecture Review*, vol.5, pp. 120-167, July 1917.

7 George Merrick, *Planning the Greater Miami – for the Tomorrows*, printed by Unanimous Resolution of the Miami Realty Board, 1937.

8 "Interview with Denise Scott Brown on 10 May 1988 in Philadelphia" in Joselita Raspi Serra, Françoise Astorg Bollack and Tom Killian, *Everyday Masterpieces – Memory and Modernity*, Edizioni Panini, Modena, 1988.

9 John Hancock, John Nolen, "New Towns in Florida 1922-29" in *The New City n⁰ 1, Foundations*, University of Miami School of Architecture, Princeton University Press, 1991.

10 Le Corbusier, *Aircraft*, The Studio, 1935 (reedition by Universe Books, New York, 1988).

11 Along with Andres Duany and Elizabeth Plater-Zyberk, the founders were Bernardo Fort-Brescia and Laurinda Spear.

12 On-site design has become the trademark of Duany & Plater-Zyberk's work under the name of *charrette*.

13 Robert Stern and John Massengale, "The Anglo-American Suburb," *Architectural Design Profile n⁰ 51*, 10/11, London, 1981.

14 Ebenezer Howard, *Garden Cities of Tomorrow*, Faber and Faber Ltd, London, 1945; Introduction by Lewis Mumford.

15 Le Corbusier, *Œuvres Complètes*, Vol. 1929-1934, p.111.

16 The Master of Architecture in Suburb and Town Design, created in 1988 at the School of Architecture of the University of Miami, is unique in the United States.

17 Francesco Dal Co, "From Parks to Region," in Dal Co, Manieri-Elia, Tafuri, et al. *The American City, from the Civil War to the New Deal*, MIT Press, 1979.

18 Richard Sennett, "The Tyrannies of Intimacy," in *The Fall of the Public Man*, pp. 339-340, Vintage Books, New York, 1976.

19 It remains to be seen when and how well Roberto Burle-Marx's original project will be realized. The 9th Street Mall, centrepiece of the ParkWest district, was made possible through the constant efforts of Jack Luft.

TROPICAL COCKTAIL

House on Palm Island,
Miami Beach, 1992.
Early sketch.
Arch: Trelles Architects.
© Trelles Architects.

THE DOMESTIC SCALE

Miami is a city of houses, a "domestic city." In this truly modern city, desperately lacking public architecture, the domestic realm and the landscape predominate in the collective eye. Houses and trees are Miami's true monuments, and even its rare public attractions — its grand hotels, the Deering Estate, the Deco District, etc. — partake of the domestic.

Miami is a city of detached houses — tens of thousands of houses, each with a front and a back garden: modest houses, in close ranks, almost urban with their second floor balconies, in Little Havana; pioneer bungalows, Mediterranean cottages and villas, pure and screened modernist volumes, and sprawling "ranchburgers," all hiding behind the lush landscapes of Coconut Grove, Miami Beach, Bayside, Miami Shores and Coral Gables; high-rise condominiums like vertical villas; and finally, the standardized "cookie-cutter" boxes and monster-houses "on steroids" — the poorly built latecomers in the suburbs of Cutler Ridge and Kendall, and not surprisingly among the major victims of Hurricane Andrew.

Like every alcoholic drink, this "Tropical Cocktail" — made up of a selected blend from "the Three Traditions" — should help us forget the mediocre reality of Miami's contemporary architecture, the pretentious shortsightedness of profit-minded clients and unconcerned public officials, and above all the absence of any serious urban consideration. Deprived of urban commissions, the "Cocktail" architects have resigned themselves to building, in Alberti's words, the "house like a small city." Ca'Ziff, the Treister Residence, Mateu House...: they all aim, beyond their "stylistic" differences, to reinvent a city house in a suburban setting. In the 1970s, Arquitectonica's Spear House opened the way to the re-examination of South Beach; fifteen years later Gianni Versace's residence on Ocean Drive (the restored Amsterdam Palace) might be considered the first — and hopefully not the last — urban palace of the city.

Miller House.
Palm Island,
Miami Beach,
1955.
Arch: Rufus Nims.
Ezra Stoller © Esto.

KENNETH TREISTER
RESIDENCE
Coconut Grove, 1958-59
Arch: Kenneth Treister

The tropical court and garden house
was built entirely of Chilean cypress.
The lot was first enclosed by a
coral wall that created an intimate
private world.
The enclosed space was then
divided into gardens,
courts, semi- and enclosed spaces
that wed man to nature.

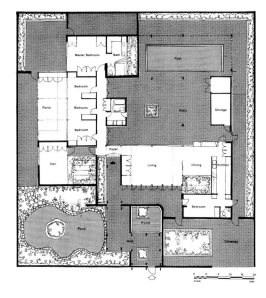

Ground floor.

Enclosed entrance garden.
© Al Barg.

Entrance view.

© Dan Forer.

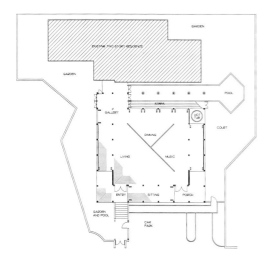

Ground floor.

A bougainvillea-covered tropical pavilion
opens completely to small private gardens.
One of them, with a pool, connects to
an old Mediterranean house.
Crafted from structure to furniture
of Brazilian *Ipe*,
its architect-designed stained glass,
copper lighting, mahogany carvings
and furniture create a total
integration of the arts.

Pool between
Ipe pavilion
and renovated
existing house.

© Dan Forer.

SULLIVANT PAVILION
Coconut Grove, 1988
Arch: Jorge Hernandez,
with Georges Pastor and Omar Morales

Exterior view.

© Jorge Hernandez.

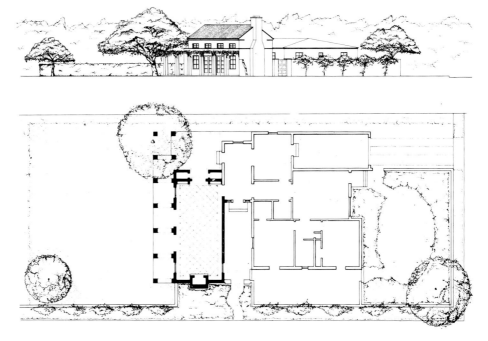

Plan.

Interior view.

© Rosanna Liebman.

An addition to an existing house,
this building contains
one single living room
which establishes
the appropriate connection
between the house
and its jungle-like landscape.

FERRÉ RESIDENCE
Coconut Grove, 1986
Arch: Zyscovich, Inc
(Bernard Zyscovich,
Joe Murguido)

The reflecting pool along
the entranceway.
© Steven Brooke.

View from the entrance.
© Steven Brooke.

A small English-style country house
was remodelled to suit the tropical
Miami climate.
The entrance sequence and the design
of the gardens
draw from Edwin Lutyens.
The roof shingles seem to match the
bark of the oaks,
and the "Tropical Tudor" style
is reinforced with the
glass-filled gable-ends.

RANCHO CAMALIZ
Redlands (South Dade), 1985
Arch: Trelles Architects,
with Juan Calvo

Oblique elevation of the stables.
Coffee wash.
© Trelles Architects.

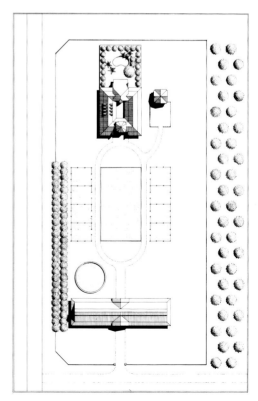

This unbuilt project
for a ranch
covers a five-acre track of farmland
near the Everglades.
Crossed in the centre
by the principal entrance,
the stables lie beneath
a large single roof,
much like the factory buildings
of the *Ingenio Union*,
an old Cuban sugar mill.
In the Caribbean tradition,
a wooden porch wraps
the whole courtyard house.

Site plan.

Model.

© Raul Pedroso/Solo.

The Florida Keys
contain an endangered ecological
balance of vegetation and wild life.
This prototype vacation house
aims at reducing the impact on the site.
Attached to the main living volume
is the "barge" with an exterior living deck
along the bedrooms.

MALE HOUSE
Coral Gables, 1989
Arch: Jorge Hernandez,
with George Pastor

A composition of two
constructive traditions:
two wood "shot-gun houses"
become the wings of this house
whose centre is a grand
masonry "room-building",
rustic and robust
in scale and finishes.

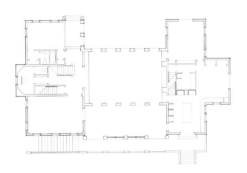

Ground floor.

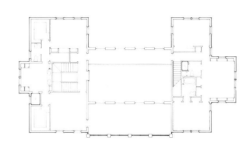

Second floor.

Street elevation.

Garden elevation.

Model.
Garden elevation.

© Jorge Hernandez.

Oblique elevation
seen from the entrance channel
to the Bay and the Port of Miami.
© Trelles Architects.

To be built on one of the
Venetian Islands in the Bay,
the house acts as a metaphor
of the Caribbean.
Facing the city,
the port and the channel entrance
for the cruise ships,
the house blends stylistic
and constructive elements
of the Haitian, Spanish colonial
and Anglo-Caribbean
traditions.

Oblique elevation seen from the
entrance channel to the Bay and the
Port of Miami, detail.
© Trelles Architects.

This house
on an island between
Miami and Key West
was designed for a scientist
and horticulturist
who required all necessary
life support systems
to be part of the project.
A paddle wheel will drive
a generator for electricity;
the roofs will collect water
which will be pumped to
a tank by a windmill;
a solar heater will heat water.
The structure is in concrete
and stainless steel.

© Charles Harrison Pawley.

COCONUT GROVE RESIDENCE
Coconut Grove, 1988
Arch: Charles Harrison Pawley

Main floor plan.

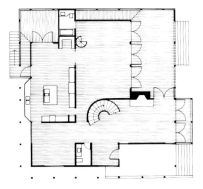

Upper floor plan.
Drawings: G. Garrone.

The ultimate Florida tropical house,
it is of Key West style with high ceilings,
paddle fans, cross ventilation,
a standing seam metal roof and wood siding.
All entertainment areas open onto
two-story high covered terraces.

View of the porch.

© Charles Harrison Pawley.

Second floor.

Ground floor.

© Trelles Architects

As a memory of urban life,
the facade on Tigertail Avenue
— an old Indian trading road —
is made up of a high wall,
with a wooden door.
All doors open on the garden
located entirely on the side
like in Charleston, South Carolina.
The concrete blocks are either
stuccoed or left exposed.
Part of the second floor is made
out of wood.

TIGERTAIL HOUSE
Miami, 1989-92.
Arch: Trelles Architects,
with Juan Calvo.

© Trelles Architects.

Street elevation.
Coffee wash.

© Trelles Architects.

COCOPLUM HOUSE I
Coral Gables, 1991
Arch: Andres Duany & Elizabeth Plater-Zyberk

West elevation.

View from the entrance toward the house and the bay.

© Raul Pedroso/Solo.

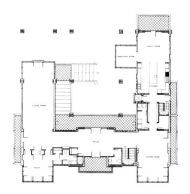

Main floor .

Upper floor .

House I is organized
around a central
and covered
courtyard,
accessible to cars
and pedestrians.

East elevation.

West elevation.

View of the house and the axial garden.
© Raul Pedrado/Solo.

House II has an asymmetrically organized plan
with a two-story breezeway
referring to its wood Cracker predecessors.
Automobiles enter in the base of the house;
the pedestrian entrance organizes
the axial gardens.

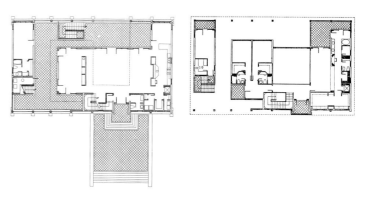

Main floor.   Upper floor.

PEREZ-GURRI HOUSE
Coral Gables, 1988-89
Arch: Jose A. Gelabert-Navia,
with Dagoberto Diaz, Rosa Navia,
Ana M. Gelabert, Nora Hurtado

This large house
is a classic example
of a "Caribbean" courtyard plan
toward which every single room
of the house is oriented.

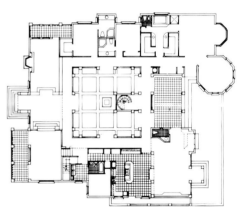

Main floor.

View from rear garden.

© Steven Brooke.

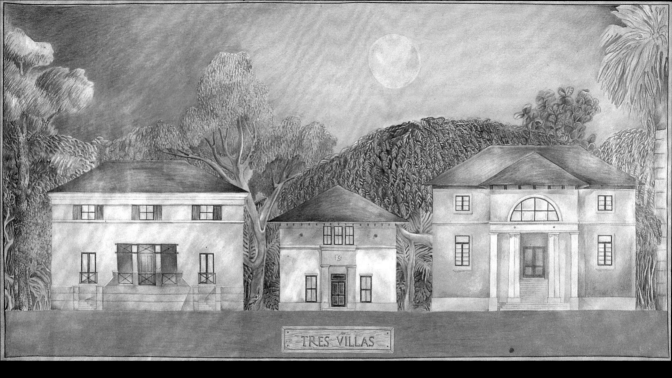

Tres Villas.
Three Palladian villas in Coral Gables.
Pencil on paper.
Arch: Jorge Hernandez,
with Francis Lynn, Ana Alvarez.

© Jorge Hernandez.

TRES VILLAS

Rear elevation with tower.

© Steven Brooke.

View from street.
© Steven Brooke.

Close to the Bay,
the house is raised
on a base containing services
and garages.
The symmetry on the street side
is disrupted by a rear tower
aligned with the intersection of two canals.
The red in the portico
comes from the flesh of the mamey,
a tropical fruit
with an ice cream-like pulp.

141

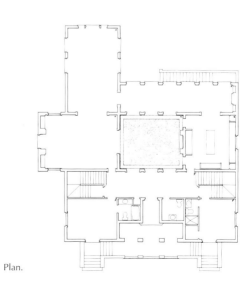

Plan.

View of the tower.

© Trelles Architects

ATRIO HOUSE
South Dade, 1989
Arch: Trelles Architects

Detail of a mahogany ceiling.

© Trelles Architects.

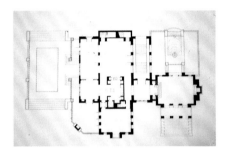

Main floor.

At the intersection of two canals,
a high tower dominates the mangroves
and marks the end of the city
and the beginning of the Keys.
A set of monumental steps
connects the base of the tower
to the living floor,
nine feet above the canal.

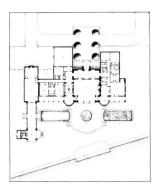

© Thomas Delbeck & M.Tedeskino.

This house is the extensive remodelling
of a "ranchburger" home built in the 50s.
The flat roofs were restructured,
and two facades were created
in an assertive way,
one on the street,
the other on the canal.

View from the canal.

© Trelles Architects.

EL PRADO HOUSE
Cocoplum, 1988
Arch: Andres Duany &
Elizabeth Plater-Zyberk,
with Raymond Chu

Corner view.
© Andres Duany & Elizabeth Plater-Zyberk.

This house is composed of two pavilions
and a open courtyard,
raised on a podium to meet flood criteria.
A sequence of entry spaces, pavilion,
stepped garden and foyer provide a
transition from street level services
to the living spaces of the second floor.

Oblique view of north elevation.
© Andres Duany & Elizabeth Plater-Zyberk.

North elevation, drawing: Jean-Pierre Majot.

Plan.

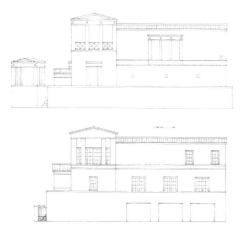

Preliminary street elevation and
street elevation as built.
Drawing: Jean-Pierre Majot.

View from the street.
© Andres Duany & Elizabeth Plater-Zyberk.

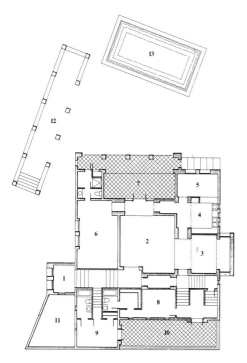

Plan

1. FOYER BELOW
2. LIVING ROOM
3. DINING ROOM
4. KITCHEN
5. BREAKFAST ROOM
6. FAMILY ROOM
7. LOGGIA
8. MAID'S ROOM
9. GUEST ROOM
10. TERRACE
11. GARDEN BELOW
12. PERGOLA
13. POOL

The house is accommodated on a podium
and is picturesquely assembled
in the manner of the Erechteum in Athens.
It is an architecture primarily
of massing to be perceived
from a specific oblique approach,
and does not depend
on craftsmanly ornament.

Red room.

Blue room.

Green room.

Yellow room.

© Teofilo Victoria and Maria de la Guardia.

CA' ZIFF
Miami, 1989-92
Arch: Teofilo Victoria and Maria de La Guardia,
with Tomas Lopez-Gottardi
Drawings: Maria de la Guardia, Teofilo Victoria

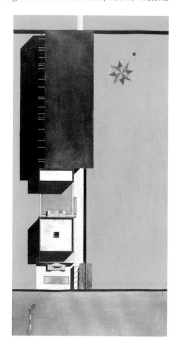

The myth of Venice lends an evocative title to the villa
and suggests a particular relationship
between the city and its geographic circumstance:
the recognition of Biscayne Bay
as the great plaza of the city.
On the bay, in the vicinity of
Villa Vizcaya, the Ca' Ziff takes
place between the mangroves
and the subtropical jungle,
and celebrates the encounter of
the Mediterranean and the Caribbean.
The main part of the house,
square in plan, contains an atrium
with a star-spangled blue ceiling.
Across the grassy court is
the guest's pavilion with its
red-stuccoed loggia on
the *piano nobile.*

Site plan.
© *Teofilo Victoria and Maria de la Guardia.*

Courtyard elevation.
© *Teofilo Victoria and Maria de la Guardia.*

147

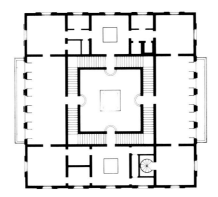

Second floor.

View of the atrium.
© Rogier Van Eck.

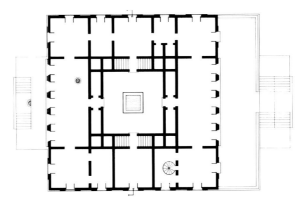

First floor.

148

© Thomas Delbeck.

Located on a quiet residential street
at the heart of Little Havana,
the architecture and urban design offices
occupy a renovated warehouse.
The main entrance displays walls
of Pompeian-red stucco and a loose curtain,
homage of the architects to their mentor, Leon Krier.

© Thomas Delbeck.

MATEU HOUSE
South Dade, 1987
Arch: Harper Carreno Mateu Sackmann, Inc

Rear oblique view of the compound.
© Raul Pedroso/Solo.

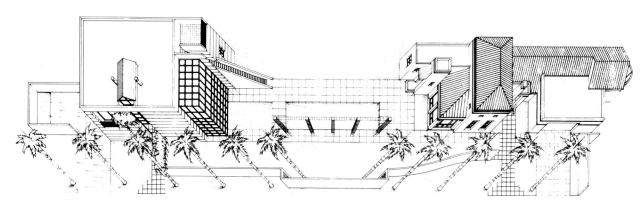

Axonometric view.

This compound of two
separate houses sharing a lot creates
a setting for an extended Cuban family.
The "front" house,
a vertical composition of flowing spaces,
is home to the architect and his young family;
the parents' "back" house
is horizontal and in more solid materials.
As the locus for the fusion of two cultures,
this old building type
infused with new meaning may
well become the domestic arrangement
of choice for a new generation
of American families.

View of the rear facade a
screened
of the "front"
© Raul Pe

HOUSE ON A 25-FOOT LOT

Coconut Grove, 1989

Arch: Harper Carreno Mateu Sackmann, Inc

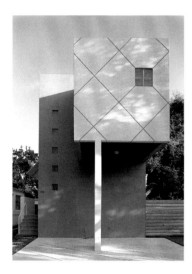

View from the street.

© Carlos Domenech.

The house is an exploration
in response to the scarcity
of land and services,
and the ever-increasing cost
of the "American Dream".
On a long and narrow lot,
unbuildable years ago
due to zoning restrictions,
a courtyard diagram
offers a sense of openness
and at the same time privacy
from its neighbors
in its compact urban setting.

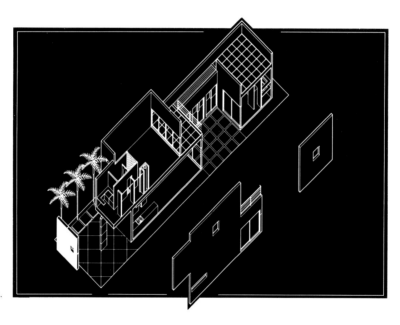

Axonometric view.

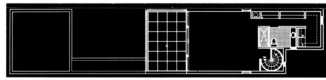

Second floor.

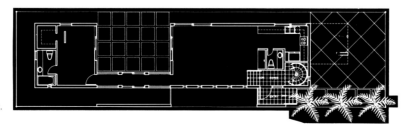

Ground floor.

The Painting Studio is an addition
to the north side of an eighty year old house
in a native Florida hammock.
The double square, east-west bar
building forms the studio.
The single cube provides canvas storage.
The six foot wide spine separates
the two volumes and serves
as a connector to the existing house.

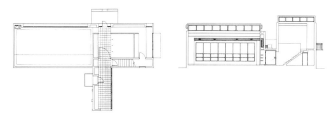

Ground floor.   Longitudinal section.

Elevation.

© Steven Brooke.

HIBISCUS HOUSE
Coconut Grove, 1980
Arch: Andres Duany &
Elizabeth Plater-Zyberk

The house recalls the period
when local classically
trained architects first encountered
European Modernism.
The plan consists
of three buildings:
a loggia, a living room and
a block of utilitarian rooms.

Perspective sketch.

View from the pool.
© Andres Duany & Elizabeth Plater-Zyberk.

Hibiscus house in Coconut Grove
detail of the front elevation
© Steven Broo

FLORIDA KEYS RESIDENCE
Florida Keys, 1974
Arch: Charles Harrison Pawley

A truly tropical island house, it was designed
to be independent of all energy sources.
It collects water that is stored in a cistern for emergency use
and has a backup generator for any loss of power.
The poured-in-place concrete two-story residence is suspended
on four concrete columns.
Three quarters of the exterior walls are glass;
they slide away into pocketed areas leaving the house
open to the surrounding screened terraces.
© Charles Harrison Pawley.

ADIA RESIDENCE
Miami, 1986
Arch: Robert Whitton

To maximize the very small
amount of land at his disposal,
the house was build
very close to the lot line
on all sides.
The basic theme
was a central spine
developed as a gradually
ascending stairway
moving back and up
through the entire structure,
the living spaces protruding
off that spine and connected
to each other by it.

© Robert Whitton

SPEAR HOUSE
Miami Shores, 1976-78
Arch: Arquitectonica International

© Arquitectonica International.

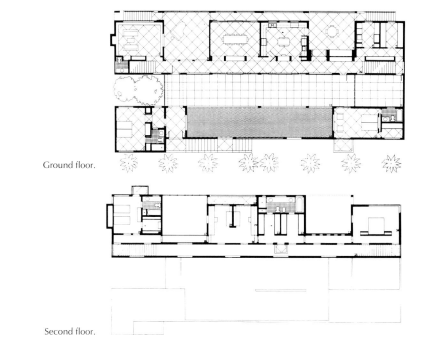

Ground floor.

Second floor.

The Spear House is intended as an
urban house in a suburban context.
The west facade, approached from the
street through a tropical grove,
faces a paved plaza
planted with palm trees.
The east facade is built on the very edge
of the water, thus addressing Biscayne Bay
in the manner of a Venetian palace on the Grand Canal.

The design of the *Acropolis*
Apartments on Brickell Avenue
makes architecture by the
juxtaposition of paradigm
and circumstance.

Elevation
on Brickell Avenue.

© Jean-François Lejeune.

ARCHITECTS OFFICES
South Miami, 1992
Arch: Robert Brown & Paul Demandt

The building transforms a banal parking
solution into a whimsical quality:
the wavy ramp of painted
concrete can be climbed
pleasantly by the motorist
and the pedestrian.
The two-story building
houses the architects;
a developer and a contractor
have offices under the ramp.
All blocks are left exposed
and painted.

View of lateral entrance.
© Jean-François Lejeune.

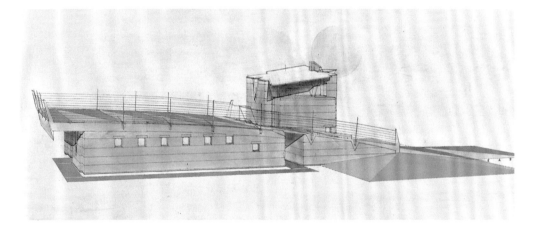

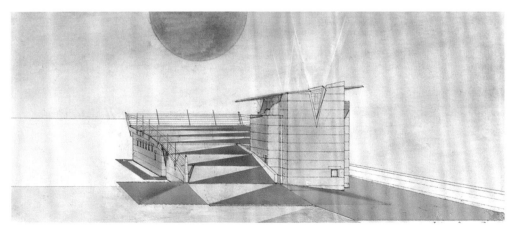

Perspective views.
© Brown-Demandt Architects.

The speed of the traffic
inspired the streamlined facade
to be viewed from
the moving car
or the metrorail.

Night view.

MAYFAIR IN THE GROVE
MAYFAIR HOUSE HOTEL
Coconut Grove, Miami, 1978-84
Arch: Kenneth Treister, with Antonio Cantillo

Drawing its architecture from Moorish, Spanish and Latin American traditions — and the Catalan Antonio Gaudi — the shopping centre is made up of courtyards, pools and luxuriant vegetation. The hotel has broad Caribbean overhangs, balconies and atria. Each room possesses a garden screened with lattice covered in bougainvillea.

Interior view of the shopping centre and hotel.
© Dan Forer.

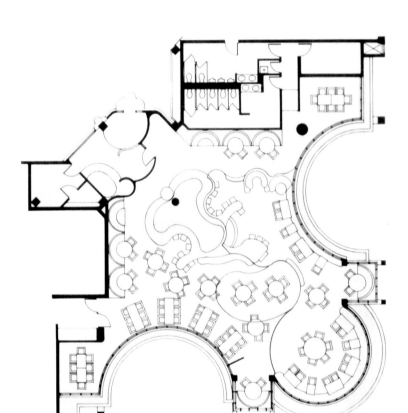

Lobby plan.

Entrance on Mayfair Lane
© Dan Forer.

Detail of a lamppost.
© Dan Forer.

THE NEW TOWN OF SEASIDE

ANDRES DUANY AND
ELIZABETH PLATER-ZYBERK,
ARCHITECTS AND TOWN
PLANNERS, MIAMI.
ROBERT DAVIS, DEVELOPER.

For the traveler driving along the Gulf of Mexico, in the Florida Panhandle, the small town of Seaside appears like a mirage at the end of a disastrous thirty mile strip of cheap motels, condominiums, concrete convenience store. The town was designed between 1978 and 1983, on an eighty acre site, along 2,300 feet of pristine beach. If Seaside is exactly the size of Leon Krier's ideal community, its density (2,000 residents when completed) and its streetscape are definitely American.

Seaside relies on typical American town design principles — detached houses, porches and fences, frontyards and backyards — but its plan is more sophisticated. The grid of streets perpendicular to the main road is lined with cottages; each street is terminated by a pavilion on the beach. From the central square, opening on the road and the open air market, three important streets radiate toward public buildings: to the west, the future town hall and conference centre; to the north, the Ruskin Square and the chapel; to the east, the diagonal Seaside Avenue terminated by a bathhouse. Also to the east, a small circular square (Tupelo Circle) marks the transition with the neighboring and uncompleted village of Seagrove.

Typologically, Seaside is unique in the United States. Beyond the traditional detached cottages, it includes: the mixed-use buildings with double-height arcades around the central square of which the prototype is found in Main Streets throughout the South, although seldor in so continuous a manner; the townhouses, inspired by Boston examples, in construction along Ruskin Square; the Antebellum houses aligned on the diagonal Seaside Avenue; and the first "Charleston-type" houses to be built outside of Charleston. All cottages are built in wood, with tin metal roofs. As for the monuments, from the beach pavilions to the future belvedere to be built by Leon Krier, they reflect the vision of Robert Davis: their intense poetic and mediatic contents have already given a true symbolic value to the foundation of the new town.

Tupelo Beach
Street Pavilion.
Arch: Ernesto Buch.
© Th. Delbeck & M. Tedeskino.

© Th. Delbeck & M. Tedeskino.

Cooper House I.
Arch: Cooper Johnson Smith.
© Th. Delbeck & M Tedeskino.

Project for a belvedere
on the central square.
Arch: Leon Krier.

© Leon Krier.

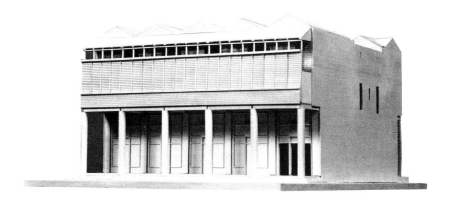

Project for a mixed-use building (retail and apartments) on the west side of the central square. The urban code mandates a double-height pedestrian arcade. Arch: Rodolfo Machado & Jorge Silvetti, 1990.

© Machado Silvetti Architects.

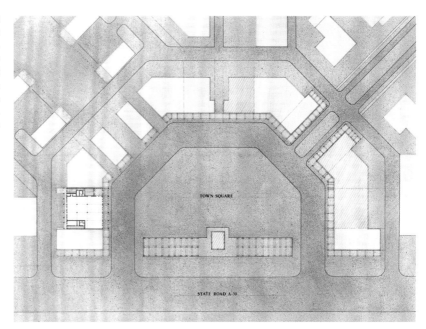

Project for a belvedere and a marketplace on the central square. Arch: Leon Krier.

© Leon Krier.

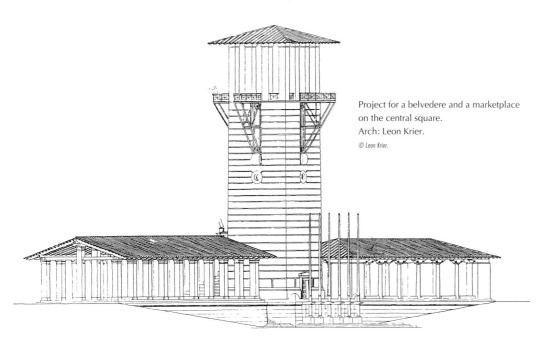

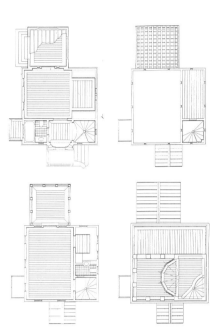

Ground floor.   Third floor.
Second floor.   Fourth floor.

Krier/Wolff House o▸
Tupelo Circle
Arch: Leon Krier, 199C
© Steven Brook

Project for
a newspaper kiosk.
Arch: Leon Krier,
with Liam O'Connor.
© Leon Krier.

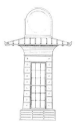

View from Tupelo Circle toward
the Gulf of Mexico.
© Steven Brooke.

Averett Tower.
Arch: Deborah Berke.
© Th. Delbeck & M. Tedeskino.

Rosewalk cottages.
© Th. Delbeck & M. Tedeskino.

HYBRID BUILDING
Arch: Steven Holl, 1989

The Hybrid Building occupies
the eastern side of the town square.
It incorporates commercial spaces on the ground floor,
offices on the second, and apartments with a shared
courtyard on the third and fourth level.
The three towers contain two-level apartments for use
by "melancholic types": a tragic poet, a musician
and a mathematician...

View of the town
from the inner
courtyard on the third floor.
© Paul Warchol.

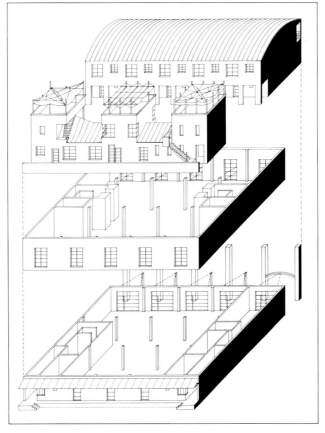

Exploded axonométric.

Perspective.

174

THE VILLAGE OF WINDSOR
VERO BEACH — FLORIDA

BY ANDRES DUANY AND
ELIZABETH PLATER-ZYBERK,
ARCHITECTS AND TOWN
PLANNERS, 1989.

Windsor is the first new village to be built in South Florida since the heyday of town-building ended in the 1920s. Public spaces and private residences are controlled by a strict urban code, inspired by the 16th-century city of St Augustine in Florida — the first Spanish colonial settlement in the United States — by 18th-century Charleston and by the small English towns in the Caribbean.

The code requires houses and continuous garden walls to be built on the property lines, defining the streets and squares closely, and forming private gardens and courtyards. Four types are typologically defined. The residences have tall windows set deep in their masonry walls, wood balconies cantilevering from above, and lush foliage spilling out over the high garden walls. In St Augustine, the Spaniards built one-story masonry homes, while in the 1700s, the British added wooden second stories with ample roof overhangs and tall shuttered windows: the houses in Windsor follow the same constructive method. Their plans are laid out to create paved and planted courts, some with swimming pools.

Windsor was designed to function as a real community, with 300 residences for a total area of 416 acres. The future heart of the community will be the two-story Village Centre shaped like a crescent containing market, stores, post office, restaurant, and a few apartments. A mall of palm trees oriented east-west, on the model of the Caribbean *paseo*, connects the crescent to the Community Hall — at the intersection of the green —and to the golf course. Within walking distance are located the other community centres: the Beach Club, the Tennis Club, the Golf Club and the Polo grandstands. Small squares are located at street intersections, public greens front civic buildings and frame vistas to the golf and the landscape of grapefruit trees.

ownhouses.
iew of the garden toward
e entrance porch.
ch: Scott Merrill,
991.
Thomas Delbeck.

The houses in the village centre
seen from the green.

© Thomas Delbeck.

A small lane bordered by
houses and high garden
walls.
© Thomas Delbeck.

Project for a
courtyard house.
Elevation on the
circular plaza.
Arch: Thomas A. Spain
& Rolando Llanes, 1990.
Drawing: Thomas A. Spain.

In Charleston,
since property owners were taxed
on their house's front footage,
the narrow portion of the house
faced the street,
while all principal rooms
had views on the side garden
enclosed by walls.
This elegant typology
will become the basic
urban component
of the Windsor block.

The citrus grove inside
the garden walls.
© Jean-François Lejeune.

SIDEYARD HOUSE
Arch: Scott Merrill, 1990-91

Angle view.
© Thomas Delbeck.

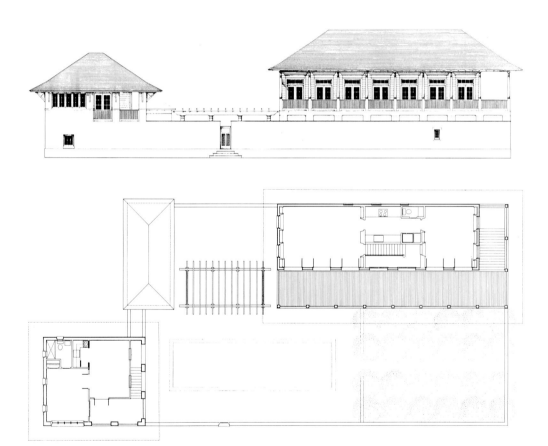

Side facade on a lane.
Second floor plan.

181

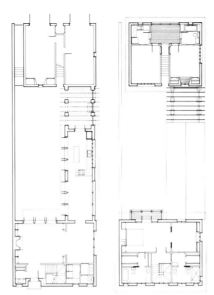

Plans of the
central house.
First floor.
Second floor.

View from
the green.
© Thomas Delbeck.

The most urban block of Windsor faces
the green toward the north.
Each house has a long garden
and an outbuilding
on the back lane,
containing a garage
and a small
apartment.

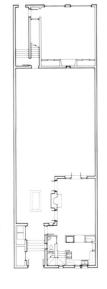
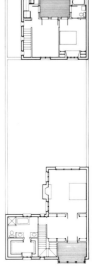

Plans of the
corner house.
First floor.
Second floor.

Facade on the green.
© Thomas Delbeck.

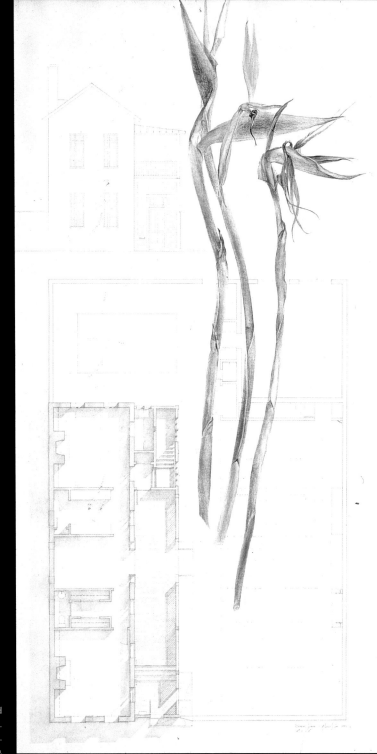

Sideyard house with bird
of paradise.
Arch: Rocco Ceo, 1990.

© Rocco Ceo.

Sideyard house.
Arch: Scott Merrill, 1990.
© Thomas Delbeck.

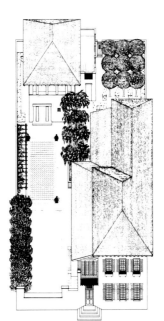

Project.
Arch: Jorge Hernandez,
Joanna Lombard and
Denis Hector, 1990.
© Jorge Hernandez, Joanna Lombard & Denis Hector.

View of the pool from the entrance porch.

© Thomas Delbeck.

Interior courtyard.
© Thomas Delbeck.

Elevation on the mall.
© Jean-François Lejeune.

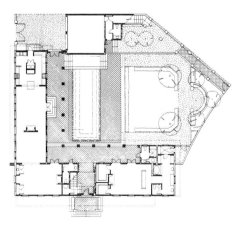

Ground floor.

Project for a sideyard house.
Side elevation.
Arch: Jorge Hernandez, Joanna Lombard
and Denis Hector.

The first houses in the village centre seen from the polo field.
© Thomas Delbeck.

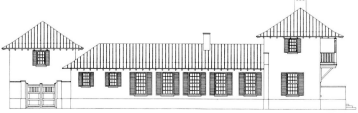

Courtyard house.
Elevation along the green.
Arch: Andres Duany & Elizabeth Plater-Zyberk.

Sideyard house.
Front elevation.
Arch: Scott Merrill.

Courtyard house.
Elevation on the mall.
Arch: Andres Duany & Elizabeth Plater-Zyberk.

A garden.
© Thomas Delbeck.

Editions Archives d'Architecture Moderne
Rue Defacqz, 14 - B-1050 Brussels

PRINTED IN BELGIUM
D/1992/1802/2
ISBN: 2-87/143-080-2